# Nurturing a SMART CHILD in this Digital Age

## A STEP-BY-STEP GUIDE TO BOOSTING YOUR CHILD'S ACADEMIC PERFORMANCE

SUJITA (MALA) N. CHATANI

INDIA • SINGAPORE • MALAYSIA

ISBN 979-8-89026-861-7

# Dedication

To my late father, Nanikram (Nanik) and
Late mother, Joti Chatani,
Without the knowledge and wisdom
They imparted to me,
I would not have written this book.
To God Almighty
Be all the glory
For His abundant goodness
And grace!

# Contents

## Part III: WHAT PARENTS SHOULD KNOW IN THIS DIGITAL AGE

# Acknowledgments

I acknowledge my father for encouraging me to write this book, my mother for believing in me and my siblings for constantly motivating me to complete this book;

My friends, Ma. Remedios K. Taguba, Angela V. Wieneke, Ruth Kwan Yap, and Elmer Beloy, for their indispensable help, support, guidance, and motivation for this book and my website, www.teachermala.com;

My mentors, John R. Pagulayan, Jon Orana, Paul Garilao, and Joseph Pagtananan, for starting and guiding me on this journey;

My editors, Marlene Legaspi-Munar, Christine Temblique, and Levy Reyes, for the valuable feedback in making this book more helpful to parents;

All my students, especially Royce Keif De Guzman and Zid Yarcia, for giving me the experience of guiding them to be a SMART CHILD;

The parents of my students for trusting and believing in me and allowing me to learn from their children;

Lastly, I thank God for giving me wisdom and guiding me in writing this book and all my life's endeavors.

# Foreword

**IS IT NATURE OR NURTURE?**

Parents and teachers like myself always ask these questions whenever our children or students perform poorly or below standard.

What could be the reason behind this? Can it be the IQ factor? Is it something we may have overlooked? As parents, we constantly search for answers. We want the best things for our children. We want to nurture our children to be SMART CHILDren.

Teacher Mala is single and has no children. She shares her wealth of experience gained from two decades as a tutor at her tutorial center, Lakshmi Learning Centre, Inc. Her teaching strategies have enabled students to excel regardless of any difficulties they encounter in school. Developing effective study habits and improving concentration are some strategies that have helped her students become more focused. Therefore, she writes with authentic wisdom.

She presents the three secrets of nurturing a SMART CHILD: Nourish Your Mind by Understanding the RECIPE Method, Get to Know Your Child by Using the SMART CHILD Tool Kit, and Motivate Your Child Using the HELP Method, which she will explain later. She validates her secrets with case studies of her successful students from her tutorial classes. Teacher Mala's tips are practical, easy to follow, and easy to implement.

The common goal is to help all children develop good values, improve concentration, and have healthy study habits. They will also learn what time management skills, organization skills, and relationship values are. All these are very relevant in our daily lives.

Also, as a bonus, the SMART CHILD Checklist benefits parents and teachers. This checklist helps parents identify their child's strengths and areas of improvement and track their child's habits.

I am grateful that this book is available now. It can be a helpful resource for parents in their quest for answers. Every parent and teacher must read this book because it is a step-by-step guide on what to do and provides practical advice and down-to-earth suggestions to help nurture a SMART CHILD. Follow the tips and see your child transform.

I wish this book was available earlier because we would have all benefited from it. Our lives would have been more manageable. I endorse this book without reservation.

You must read it, apply it, and watch your child flourish.

Rtaguba

**DR. REMEDIOS K. TAGUBA**

FORMER REGIONAL DIRECTOR, DEPARTMENT OF EDUCATION

Cordillera Administrative Region,

The administrator of Ridgeview Academy Baguio

# Preface

**BEFORE YOU BEGIN READING THIS BOOK...**

Dear Parents/Guardians,

You made a wise decision when you purchased this book. You are concerned about the welfare of your child. This book can change your child's future.

Parents, if your children are born in this digital age, you must be facing significant challenges. Your children spend most of their day on social media, watching television, or playing computer games. Are you aware of the severe detrimental effects it has on your children? It distracts them from studying. Also, it paves the way for a life that lacks discipline.

Since you know your children lack discipline, you must act immediately. In the beginning, you will find it very tedious. You will notice that it becomes much easier and more manageable when you practice it consistently.

I am a teacher, and I run a tutorial center. I listen to parents' problems daily and realize they have similar concerns about discipline. They need help finding solutions to their problems because there are no answers in books or on the internet.

Parents urgently need a guide to help solve their pressing concerns. So, I documented all my experiences and compiled them into a book to help parents address their problems.

The strategies in this book have raised thousands of SMART CHILDren. I have raised doctors, engineers, pilots, lawyers, musicians, teachers, etc.

This book's basis is how my parents nurtured my siblings and me to be SMART CHILDren. They were able to raise three scholars. This book is a tribute to my dear, departed parents.

God has given me the gift of nurturing children. I enjoy touching their lives and unleashing their potential. I train them to master the basics and excel at school. Most of my students have received academic excellence awards. I am very proud of them.

This book aims to guide parents to raise well-rounded, responsible, independent, and confident children. I talk about real-life situations and share practical solutions for every situation.

I divided the book into three parts:

- **Part One** talks about how I became a teacher. It also discusses how the concept of a SMART CHILD originated and the discovery of the three secrets.
- **Part Two** discusses the secrets: Nourish Your Mind by Understanding the RECIPE Method, Get to Know Your Child by Using the SMART CHILD Tool Kit, and Motivate Your Child Using the HELP Method.
- **Part Three** talks about what every parent must do in this digital age. It also discusses managing your child's use of gadgets and improving focus or concentration. It guides you on how to start, implement the strategies and eventually teaches you how to build an encouraging home life.

This book applies to children but is also relevant to adults searching for a path toward success. It is a powerful guide because:

- **It works fast.** The minute you implement the first secret, you will see visible changes in your child.

- **It costs nothing.** The prescribed step-by-step action plan is free. You must implement it properly and follow it until you see a difference in your child.
- **It allows you to be creative.** You can creatively implement these strategies to make them work for your child.
- **It is timeless.** Many parents have used these tried, tested, and proven secrets for generations. It worked for my grandparents, my parents, and me. It will work for you and your child as well.

Let me offer you some caution and a gentle reminder:

After the end of every chapter, pause and implement what you have read. Implementation is the key. You may need to make some adjustments. You can contact me if you experience any challenges, and I will guide you.

This system will work very well for mainstream children. However, it may also work for differently-abled children, provided they can follow. It will be very challenging, but it is possible.

It will not be easy, but you must be consistent, patient, dedicated, and persevering. You must believe in it 100%. Also, you must do whatever it takes to implement it successfully. Ideally, you need to PUSH and make it work.

Bear in mind that your child will not transform overnight. There is no shortcut. Forming positive habits takes time. It will help if you become very patient. I am here to hold your hand along the way.

Why am I saying this? I want you to benefit from the book. I am very passionate and serious about training your child. I can only help you if you are 100% committed and willing to apply everything this book prescribes. Remember, if you are ready to commit, you must do it all the way.

In the following pages, you will discover the secrets that will transform your child. You must read this book from cover to cover instead of skimming through the pages or jumping from one section to another.

Since I am not a parent, some may say I am not an expert in nurturing children. Over the past two decades, I have helped transform thousands of students, even the most challenging ones. My love for children prevents me from turning away challenging students. There is no child I cannot handle.

If you are experiencing problems not listed in this book and need help, please visit the website www.teachermala.com. Please fill in the contact form, and I'll reply soon. Happy reading!

Yours sincerely,

*Teacher Mala*

Part One

# MY JOURNEY

CHAPTER ONE

# My Story

My teaching career was not an accident. God led me to the teaching path. Let me share how I transformed from Princess Mala to Teacher Mala.

## My Transformation from Princess Mala to Teacher Mala

*Life was not easy for our family. My parents came from a middle-income background and had difficulty making ends meet. They had a hand-to-mouth existence and had no money for tutoring. Yet, they nurtured three SMART CHILDren who earned scholarship awards.*

*Hi! I am Mala Chatani, an Indian girl born and raised in Manila, Philippines, but I grew up in Jakarta and Singapore. I have two older siblings, ten and eight years older. Since I am the youngest, I was considered the family's princess.*

*Due to the large age gap, my sisters excluded me from all their activities. They would ignore me and play with their friends. As a result, I developed an inferiority complex. I became shy and quiet, and I hardly had any friends.*

*When I was seven, my family and I moved from Manila to Jakarta. I was much happier because my situation changed for the better. My parents enrolled me in an Indian co-ed school; I adjusted quickly, and my grades improved tremendously. I made many friends, and we are still in touch today.*

*After five years, my family and I relocated from Jakarta to Singapore because of visa problems. It was a massive adjustment for me. I studied at a Chinese public school that had a very different environment. I could not blend in because of language differences; I could not understand them since they mostly spoke in Chinese. I could feel they were talking about me. Sometimes, they made fun of me. I reacted by overeating, and my grades started slipping.*

*The school principal had to call my parents' attention. My father was so worried. He knew I was suffering emotionally, so he decided to help me. My father and I would sit together every morning to review the previous day's lessons. He patiently explained the topics I did not understand.*

*Gradually, my grades improved, and I received the "Best Progressive Student" award and a scholarship from the school. It boosted my self-esteem, and I became more confident because name-calling and bullying stopped.*

*After four years, the family needed to return to Manila. After adjusting to the British education system, I had to adapt to the American education system. This time, I felt encouraged. I knew I could adapt if my parents were willing to help me.*

*My parents enrolled me in Assumption College, Makati. I received a Bachelor of Arts degree, majoring in Economics. Then I worked for Landmark Corporation as a credit clerk for two years. There, I developed a passion for computers. My father encouraged me to pursue a computer-related degree. I decided to take a Master's degree in Information Management at Ateneo Professional School. I transferred to First DataCorp and worked as a computer programmer for six years.*

*One day, while at work, I received a call informing me that my mother had fractured her hip. I decided to resign and take care of her. I also helped my father with his T-shirt business.*

*I needed to grow professionally after seven years of working with my father. I did not know what to do. I kept praying to the Lord for guidance on what to do until the Lord led me to teach.*

*One afternoon, I went to the village clubhouse to mail a letter. As I waited in line, I met this Indian-looking man holding a stack of flyers. He came up to me and struck up a conversation. Then, he gave me a brochure and asked me to apply for a position at his mother's school.*

*The following day, I headed to the school's Makati Village campus to apply, which was their preschool campus. The owner's daughter interviewed me. Then, she sent me to the grade school campus, the main campus, where the school owner interviewed me. Before I realized it, I had landed a computer teacher job.*

*I discovered that working as a teacher was a tough job. The students did not listen to me. I struggled and wanted to give up, but a kind co-teacher showed me what to do. These are some of the most valuable pieces of teaching advice she gave me:*

- ***Understand** your students*
- ***Know** them*
- ***Bond** with them and learn to connect*

*After following this advice, I became a much better teacher. My students understood me and got better grades, and I became happier.*

*The teaching field opened up so many opportunities for me. As a franchisee of an educational method, I learned how to nurture my students. After two and a half years, I converted it into a tutorial center.*

*In 2012, I wrote and published a book titled "Discipline Your Child" under the name Laxmi Mitra. It opened up a new opportunity because a publisher invited me to write Math textbooks.*

*In 2015, I became a textbook author for Glad Tidings Publishing. I wrote the Math preschool books (Nursery, Kindergarten, and Prep Levels) under the Math Applied for Zeal and Excellence (MAZE) Series. I also wrote the Grade 4 level of this series in early 2020.*

*During the pandemic, I converted my tutorial center into an online learning program called SMART Academic Hack. It is a one-on-one tutorial program where I ensure every child learns the basics. Currently, I teach over 100 students, including students with special needs. Every child is an achiever, and no child is difficult to handle. I am very passionate about nurturing SMART CHILDren. My tutorial center is known for its quality. "You just have to know how to unleash your child's potential," I tell the parents. Due to my life experiences, I can understand how a child feels. My vision is to "Make a difference in every child's life."*

*Mala Chatani, a shy and quiet girl, transformed into a SMART CHILD and a confident teacher. Teacher Mala helps busy or struggling parents raise academic achievers by increasing their child's attention span using THE SMART CHILD Method.*

Every child struggles at some point in their life. Some children may overcome their struggles independently, while others may need help. You are not alone on this journey.

When it comes to nurturing a SMART CHILD or unleashing your child's potential, my two decades of teaching experience have made me a true advocate. If your child or your friend's child:

- Watches more than two hours of television every day
- Spends more than two hours playing on digital devices
- Cannot focus
- Gets low grades in school

You can contact me via email at **help@teachermala.com.** I am willing to help. I can help you with the following:

- Develop your child's study habits.
- Limit your child's access to gadgets and television.
- Teach your child to focus on and excel at one task.
- Instill discipline in your child.

Remember, every problem has a solution. Let us avoid getting stuck with the issues and focus on finding solutions. Let us unleash your child's potential and bring out their most vital traits by nurturing them to be SMART CHILDren.

**Points to Ponder:**

- ❑ Every child struggles at some point in their life.
- ❑ Every problem has a solution. Let us focus on finding solutions.
- ❑ As a parent, you can unleash your child's potential using the methods prescribed in this book.

CHAPTER TWO

# What Is A SMART CHILD?

Parents and guardians, you are responsible for your child's future. The way you nurture your child will shape your child's future. If you want your child to have a bright future, train him to be a SMART CHILD.

A child has four quotients: The Intelligence Quotient (IQ), the Emotional Quotient (EQ), the Social Quotient (SQ), and the Adversity Quotient (AQ). Below is an explanation of each quotient:

1. The **Intelligence Quotient (IQ)** measures your ability to understand or comprehend, solve math problems, memorize things, and recall topics. You get to use your brain intelligently.
2. The **Emotional Quotient (EQ)** measures your ability to maintain peace with others; be punctual, responsible, and honest. It teaches you to respect boundaries and be humble, genuine, and considerate. It guides you to feel things using your emotions.
3. The **Social Quotient (SQ)** measures your ability to make friends, build a network, and maintain long-lasting relationships.
4. The **Adversity Quotient (AQ)** measures your ability to go through a challenging time and come out of it without losing your mind.

A child is well-balanced when all four quotients are at the same level.

SMART CHILD, in terms of Intelligence Quotient (IQ), means your child is intelligent, gets high grades in school, and answers questions spontaneously.

SMART CHILD, in terms of Emotional Quotient (EQ), Social Quotient (SQ), and Adversity Quotient (AQ), is an acronym for:

**S** – Sociable

**M** - Motivated

**A** – an Achiever

**R** - Responsible

**T**- Trustworthy

**C** – Creative

**H** – Happy

**I** – Independent

**L**- Lovable

**D** - Dedicated

**The formula of a SMART CHILD:**

$$IQ = EQ + AQ + SQ$$

**Does my child need to have all these qualities?**

You may think your child must have all these qualities, but that is not necessarily true. Your child may possess one or two traits, but he will develop these traits as he goes through the RECIPE Method. Sometimes it may even take years to instill this in him.

## Example of a SMART CHILD

Every well-balanced child possesses these characteristics. Let me share the story of one of my students, Ivan, who became a well-balanced child.

*I am Ivan, a Grade Five student at Don Bosco, Makati. I enjoy playing computer games and watching television. When I come home from school, the first thing I do is eat. Then, I rest and watch television for about 30 minutes. I call my mother to inform her of all my assignments for the day.*

*My mother is a working mom who cannot spend too much time with me. She requires me to do all my assignments independently. When I don't understand what to do, I ask for her help. Then, I review the lessons for the day. If I finish early, I can watch more television or do whatever I want, provided I go to bed by 9:00 p.m. to wake up on time the following day.*

*On Fridays, I rest and do whatever I want. On Saturday mornings, I review at least two subjects for the week. After studying, I participate in extracurricular activities. In the evening, I continue reviewing the other subjects. I go to church on Sunday mornings and spend time with my family After lunch, I make sure I finish all my school preparations to be ready for Monday.*

*I sleep early on Sunday night to be refreshed and recharged for Monday.*

In Ivan's story, you will notice he has the qualities of a SMART CHILD. Let us summarize these qualities:

1. Ivan is **sociable (friendly)**. He has many friends and **socializes** by joining extra-curricular activities.

2. Ivan is **motivated**. When Ivan comes home from school, **he studies and does his homework independently**. He does not need any pushing, but his mother checks on him.
3. Ivan is an **achiever.** He **makes sure he achieves the targets he has set for himself.**
4. Ivan is **responsible**. He follows a **daily** routine, and he knows what to do.
5. Ivan is **trustworthy**. Ivan's mother **does not have to remind him what to do**. She trusts Ivan that he will finish all his tasks. All she has to do is check with him.
6. Ivan is **creative**. He comes up with different ways to achieve a goal.
7. Ivan is **happy**. He is content with his life.
8. Ivan is **independent**. He can do things without being pushed.
9. Ivan is **lovable**. Everyone likes or loves Ivan because he is pleasant.
10. Ivan is **dedicated**. Even though the task is challenging, Ivan makes sure he completes it.

Based on the above story, Ivan is a SMART CHILD. A SMART CHILD is a disciplined child. Therefore, if you want your child to be successful in life, you need to teach your child discipline.

The word discipline scares many parents because they find it very harsh. Discipline is often mistaken to mean punishment. In reality, parents fail to understand the true meaning of discipline.

Based on my research, discipline comes from two Latin words, ***discipulus***, meaning pupil, and ***discere,*** meaning to learn. Therefore, the word discipline refers to teaching, guiding, or training. I will use these words interchangeably in this book.

Research shows that social media influence, technological advancements, or other digital advancements can be addictive.[1] Children spend too much time watching television, using social media, playing online games, accessing websites, sharing photos, and recording or watching videos. These can cause children to lead a life that lack discipline, if not appropriately managed. Why? Online, they only see curated realities, created by people with vested interests. Many content creators cherry-pick facts to fit their narratives.

Parents, it is your responsibility to teach or guide your child to lead a life of discipline. It means you need to teach your child how to manage gadget time.

If you are too busy working and making ends meet, you will have little time for your children. When you come home, you are too exhausted to interact; you hardly have time to check on your child's progress in school. To appease your children and your guilt, you will give into your child's whims without a second thought.

What will happen when you experience a problem? Stay calm because help is within reach. This book will guide you in instilling positive values in your child and advise you on what to do in times of need.

It will help train your child to be **S**ociable, **M**otivated, an **A**chiever, **R**esponsible, **T**rustworthy, **C**reative, **H**appy,

---

1. LeeHealth, https://www.leehealth.org/health-and-wellness/healthy-news-blog/mental-health/are-you-addicted-to-social media#:~:text=Using%20social%20media%20can%20lead,in%20neurological%20and%20physiological%20functioning, July 22, 2022.

**I**ndependent, **L**ovable, and **D**edicated. In short, this book gives you hope.

Would you like to know how many qualities your child has? Please use the SMART CHILD Checklist below.

## The Smart Child Checklist

The SMART CHILD Checklist is a checklist that will help you determine if your child has all the ten qualities of a SMART CHILD. It is essential to evaluate your child so that you will know your child's strengths and areas for improvement. You will know where to focus before you begin training your child. Always start with the positive and work on the areas for improvement.

## How to Use the Smart Child Checklist

Before you proceed, here are some guidelines you need to follow:

1. Observe your child for at least three days before you answer the checklist.
2. While answering the checklist, be truthful. It will enable you to identify if your child has the characteristics of a SMART CHILD.
3. Remember that your child is human; he is not perfect. It is usual for him to have a few of these characteristics. The idea is to identify and develop it.

## The Smart Child Checklist

### SOCIABLE

- ❑ Can your child make friends easily?
- ❑ Does your child enjoy being with friends?
- ❑ Does your child have at least 10 friends?

### CREATIVE

- ❑ Does your child come up with new ideas?
- ❑ Does your child come up with different solutions to solve a problem?
- ❑ Does your child like to ask a lot of questions?

### MOTIVATED

- ❑ Does your child do things by himself?
- ❑ Do you need to push your child to do things?
- ❑ Does your child show enthusiasm when doing an activity?

### HAPPY

- ❑ Is your child always in a good mood and smiling?
- ❑ Does your child show interest and pleasure in an activity he has chosen?
- ❑ Is your child happy to connect/keep in touch with friends?

### ACHIEVER

- ❑ Is your child able to achieve the targets or goals set?
- ❑ Does your child get easily frustrated about achieving the goal?
- ❑ Does your child work patiently to achieve the targets?

### INDEPENDENT

- ❑ Do you have to push or force your child to do tasks?
- ❑ Do you have to remind your child to do things?
- ❑ Does your child do things on his own or with little supervision?

### RESPONSIBLE

- ❑ Does your child ask what needs to be done?
- ❑ Does your child finish the task on time?
- ❑ Does your child make sure all tasks are completed on schedule despite challenges?

### LOVABLE

- ❑ Does your child have a positive outlook in life?
- ❑ Does your child show genuine interest in others?
- ❑ Is your child pleasant and easy to like?

### TRUSTWORTHY

- ❑ Does your child follow rules and instructions even if you're not around?
- ❑ Does your child tell lies?
- ❑ Does your child keep his promise?

### DEDICATED

- ❑ Does your child make excuses to avoid doing a task?
- ❑ Does your child try even if the task is difficult?
- ❑ Does your child do his best to complete a task?

**After answering the Smart Child Checklist:**

1. Count the number of checks you have on the checklist and tally up all the scores. That will be your child's score.
2. Then fill in the blanks: My child's total score is ________.
3. Analyze your child's score using the following:

   **0-10:** Skills are beginning to develop

   **10-25:** Needs Guidance

   **25-30:** Has qualities of a SMART CHILD

   The total score tells you how your child is doing.

   My child's score is _____.

   It means that my child ______________________.

4. If you need my help, email or PM me on Facebook.

   Email: help@teachermala.com or PM: Mala Chatani

**Points to Ponder:**

- ❑ A SMART CHILD is a balanced child.
- ❑ A balanced child is a disciplined child.
- ❑ A balanced child is Sociable, Motivated, an Achiever, Responsible, Trustworthy, Creative, Happy, Independent, Lovable, and Dedicated.

CHAPTER THREE

# The Discovery of the Three Secrets

*Maria, an only child and a Grade One student, is enrolled in my tutorial center. In her previous day's assignment, she had many mistakes. So, one of my teachers asked Maria to correct her work. She refused, but the teacher insisted she must do it. Maria yelled at the teacher, saying, "You are annoying!" The teacher turned to the headteacher for assistance, but the same thing happened. They approached me, and I took over and made Maria comply.*

When Maria told the teachers, "You are annoying!" they did not take it personally because they understood that Maria was just a child and they needed to be patient with her. However, they felt ineffective and unappreciated.

I immediately called for a meeting with Maria's parents, but only the father attended. During the meeting, I learned that Maria was an only child and her parents had a hectic schedule. Maria's parents always gave in to her wishes to compensate for the lost time spent with her without realizing they missed opportunities to teach Maria about respect. They will recognize this when Maria is older and regret it.

The meeting ended with no definite conclusion. I was confused, and I needed to consult a friend from the teaching field. When I got home, I called a friend who is a teacher living in Hong Kong. I told her what had happened. Frustrated, I yelled, "If I were to write a book about my life experiences, it would be helpful, and many people would benefit." All she said was, "Why don't you?" I hung up and began conceptualizing this book. I started writing this book, which led to the discovery of *Nurturing A Smart Child In This Digital Age: A Step-By-Step Guide To Boosting Your Child's Academic Performance.*

## The Three Secrets in Nurturing A SMART CHILD

Below is a detailed description of the three secrets to nurturing a SMART CHILD.

## SECRET # 1: Nourish Your Mind Using the RECIPE Method

The RECIPE Method consists of six chapters. Each chapter explains one particular stage in detail, its meaning, importance, and how to implement it. Before you proceed, you need to understand what the RECIPE Method is all about.

The RECIPE Method is a process your child must follow to become a SMART CHILD. This process comprises six stages: Routine, Empathy, Communication, Interest, Perseverance, and

Esteem. The figure illustrates the stages of becoming a SMART CHILD.

Your child must pass through each stage. Also, in each step, your child will develop the necessary skills, values, or habits before she moves on to the next step. It will mold your child to be a better person.

Why do I say this? It is because I have experienced it. In every stage, I shared many struggles, and after developing the necessary skills and good habits, I adjusted and moved on to the next step.

Every stage molded me into a better person. I learned to become an achiever. I will explain all this in detail in the succeeding chapters.

## SECRET # 2: Get to Know Your Child Using the SMART CHILD Tool Kit

Now that you understand the RECIPE Method, the next step is to get to know your child using the SMART CHILD Tool Kit. The SMART CHILD Tool Kit includes worksheets to help you understand your child and track their habits. Ensure you answer all the worksheets before doing the SMART CHILD Habit Tracker. The SMART CHILD Habit Tracker will help you implement this method by monitoring your child's habits. Before you attempt this, you need to answer the SMART CHILD Checklist.

This chapter contains a list of 50 habits your child needs to develop. You must choose, practice, and implement it for 90 days. When implementing the habit, you need to track the pattern using the tracker. Once your child is comfortable, you must follow the routine for 90 days. Then, implement the next habit until you implement all 50.

You are training your child to have good habits until your child reaches the stage of building self-esteem. At this stage, your child is independent. I will explain all this in detail in the succeeding chapters.

## SECRET # 3: Motivate Your Child Using the HELP Method

Motivation is an essential part of nurturing a SMART CHILD. With motivation, it will be easier to get your child's cooperation. Your child needs to have the drive to get what she wants.

In the HELP Method, I talk about my father's two approaches to motivating me. They are:

1. **Extrinsic Motivation**: This is the external way of motivating your child. It involves rewarding your child materially when she has completed a task and has done an excellent job.
2. **Intrinsic Motivation**: This is the internal way of motivating your child. Your child does the task voluntarily without being pushed.

In this chapter, I will teach you how to nurture your child, from motivating her extrinsically to intrinsically. Once your child becomes self-motivated, she will gradually become an academic achiever.

Below is an illustration of the HELP Method. It explains what the method is all about.

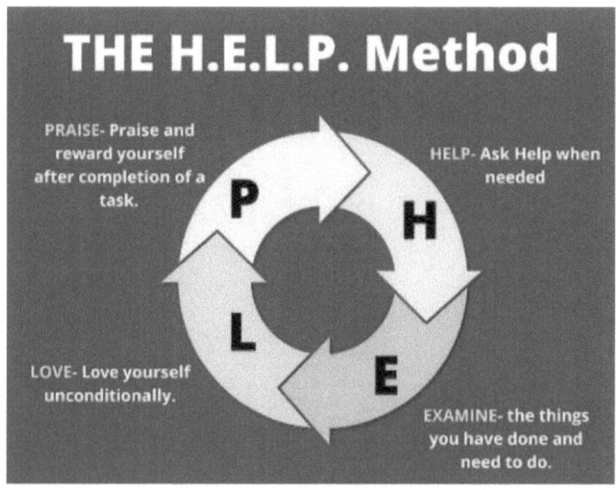


We will discuss this further in the succeeding chapters. In the next chapter, I will discuss how you can lay the foundation of a SMART CHILD.

**Points to Ponder:**

- There are three secrets to nurturing a SMART CHILD.
- These secrets are
  - SECRET # 1: Nourish Your Mind by Understanding the RECIPE Method.
  - SECRET #2: Get to Know Your Child Using the SMART CHILD Tool Kit.
  - SECRET # 3: Motivate Your Child Using the HELP Method.
- Your child's cooperation is very essential in nurturing a SMART CHILD.
- Motivation will help your child cooperate.

CHAPTER FOUR

# Laying the Foundation for a SMART CHILD

Before implementing the three secrets, you must understand the importance of nurturing a SMART CHILD. Understanding the process will keep you focused and committed to your goal.

Let me share something I learned from my dad. Decades ago, I told my father I wanted to get high grades in school. He asked me three questions: 1) Why am I studying? 2) Do I want to maintain my scores, or 3) Do I want to get higher grades? He told me that I needed to identify my objectives first. Having a clear goal is very important.

Once I identified my objective, my father asked me why I wanted to get high grades. Is it because I want to excel in school? Or is it to prove that I am not dumb? I must repeatedly ask the same questions until I find the root cause and more compelling reasons behind my motivation.

He told me that knowing the WHAT (the goal I want to achieve), knowing the WHY (the reason behind this goal), and the WHICH (the study method I am going to use) will help me commit more to a challenging task. The more precise the reason, the more I will stick to my studies. Remember, clarity sparks action.

Once you understand the reason behind your what and why, it will be easier for you to take action, and motivation will come naturally. Then, explain it to your child. Now, it will be easier to break down the details to a level your child will understand.

Let us learn about the benefits of nurturing your child to be a SMART CHILD.

## Benefits of Nurturing A SMART CHILD

What was Ivan's mother's single and most powerful action to help him excel in school? It was to train or instill discipline in him. My father explained that when he instilled discipline in me, I experienced many benefits. Here are some benefits of teaching your child to be disciplined:

1. **Your child will develop life skills.** Life skills are a set of necessary values, attitudes, or habits a child needs to succeed.

   **These skills include:**

   - decision-making and problem-solving;
   - creative and critical thinking;
   - communication and interpersonal skills;
   - self-awareness and empathy;
   - assertiveness; and
   - resilience and coping with emotions and stress.

   Let me give you a simple example. All children must learn basic housekeeping skills like cooking a simple meal, making the bed, cleaning the house, and washing and ironing the clothes. We all must learn to keep our homes tidy to ensure order and good health.

   Start with small tasks like setting the table and bringing dishes to the sink. While training your young child, please do not focus on the spills or plates breaking. Also, do not obsess about speed or tidiness. Remember, your child is under training.

Our helper helps us keep our house clean, but what happens when the helper decides to leave? Would you and your child mope and cry? No, we do not always experience good times. Expect to experience tough times too.

In tough times, what usually comes to the rescue? Life skills do. Life skills will help your child cope with all the challenges that will come his way. If you teach your child the simple skills of maintaining a house, your child will be able to handle such a situation later.

Give your child the independence to experiment while in the kitchen or doing house chores. Allow your child to be creative when learning tasks.

Your child will never learn if you let him take the easy way out. Let your child experience hardship so that he will get the opportunity to do things independently.

2. **Your child will learn how to decide wisely**. Your child will learn to make decisions objectively based on what is beneficial and necessary for him, like choosing clothes or books to read. Let him choose what he likes, and then tell him what you think is best.
3. **You will develop a nurturing parent-child relationship.** It is a unique bond that creates fruitful and lasting memories. Bond with your child and let him enjoy his childhood from a very young age. It is essential for building your child's foundation.

Also, it will influence the type of personality your child will develop and the behavior he will demonstrate. Let your child enjoy his childhood by creating memories through play opportunities like running in the park, riding a bicycle, flying a kite, or playing hide and seek, not just virtual games. Also, introduce your child to the beauty of simple street games.

4. **You will build the right relationship with your child.** Your child should enjoy being with you and not hesitate to confide in you. He must not fear you because you can be his friend too. Remember to be consistently firm but kind at all times. Encourage this relationship through loving but honest conversations.

   Also, keep your word. Your child will never believe you if you don't mean what you say.

5. **You will have opportunities to teach your child to do the right thing.** From a very young age, correct your child immediately if he does something wrong. Make sure you explain things clearly so he will avoid repeating the mistake. For example, when your child speaks impolitely to elders, correct him. Explain to him that this is disrespectful. It will be best to be mindful of how you treat others because your child will pick up cues from what he sees in his environment.

6. **Your child will learn good habits.** If your child has good habits, family members, friends, and the people around him will love and respect him. However, if he has bad habits, life will be miserable for those around him.

7. **Your child will establish a healthy balance in life.** Too much of everything is harmful. Your child must learn to balance studies, play, and extra-curricular

activities. Having a healthy balance will build a firm foundation in his character. Please note that your role as a parent is to guide him in every way. If you don't, your child will grow entitled and unable to adjust to life's imperfections.

8. **Your child will learn how to set priorities.** First, teach your child to do the most important things and the rest later. He will learn to make good decisions based on his priorities and preferences in life.

9. **You will help unleash your child's potential.** When you develop your child's study habits, you will train him to be independent and teach him good habits. It may be challenging initially, but you must consistently work on it.

## Dealing With an Undisciplined Child

Have you ever imagined how it would feel to live with an undisciplined child? Let me share a true-to-life story of a rebellious student I nurtured at my tutorial center.

A parent called me one morning and told me she urgently wanted to meet me. She said,

> *Teacher, I need help with my son, Jason. I cannot pinpoint what is wrong with him. My son is a fifth-grade student who I assume should be responsible.*
>
> *When he goes to school, he does not listen to the teacher. He does not copy notes or assignments. If he does copy, it is incomplete. When he comes home from school, he watches T.V. or plays computer games.*

*When I come home, I follow up on his studies. Then, he starts doing his homework and studying for his test. I get angry and scold him, but it does not affect him. Teacher, what should I do?*

Imagine if you had a child who displayed such behavior. It is very challenging for you to deal with. In the case of Jason's mother, she found Jason's behavior very demanding. She felt living with Jason was unpleasant because he displayed selfish behavior. He ensured he got what he wanted even if his mother felt miserable.

So, what did I tell Jason's mother? I suggested that she:

1. **Please find out the root cause of his behavior.**
    - Does Jason have a problem at school? Is he being bullied?
    - Does he have a problem at home? Is there a health issue?

2. **Make the expectations clear to him.**
    - Jason must understand what his mother expects of him and explain the reasons behind her expectations so that it will be clear.

3. **Help Jason develop a daily study routine.**
    - Jason's mother must create a daily study plan and implement it consistently. The routine should have time for both study and play.

4. **Explain the consequences.**

   ○ Jason's mother must explain that he will face the consequences if he does not follow the routine. She should also explain why she will withhold all the activities he enjoys most. However, if he completes all his tasks, he can do whatever he likes.

5. **Explain the reasons.**

   ○ Once Jason understands why she will withhold all activities he enjoys most, it will help prevent Jason from repeating the same mistake. Also, it will encourage him to complete all assigned tasks on time.

6. **Motivate your child.**

   ○ As Jason improves, his mother slowly lets him do what he enjoys most. It will serve as motivation. Also, this is one way of managing Jason's distractions.

Handling this situation was very fruitful. Soon, Jason's mother noticed a gradual transformation in her son. Today, he excels in school, and she is very proud of him.

If your child is in a similar situation, all you have to do is guide your child appropriately and bring him back on track.

Stop and assess the situation. Try to understand why your child is not performing well and find a possible solution. Then guide your child. If necessary, show disappointment because it means you are expressing that you are upset about not meeting your standard. Be honest about your feelings but never blame your child. When communicating, use the correct language to ensure you are coming from a place of help and are finding a way to improve things. It is best to discuss your standards clearly so that he will try to meet them, but at the same time, structures must be in place to ensure your child's success.

## When Should You Start?

The best piece of advice I received:

**"Instilling discipline in your child is a must."**

The question is, when is the best time to start? Based on observation, most parents begin training their children after age seven. Is that the correct age?

My father always told me, "You should begin disciplining your child from age two." He believes it is the ideal age, but many parents feel it is too early.

It is the perfect age to train your child because he will follow you blindly until it becomes his way of life. It gives you an early head start.

However, if you start at seven, it can become stressful because your child has enough faculties to reason, think, and decide for himself.

After age seven, you might already experience resistance. Resistance means going against your will. Your child refuses to do the tasks you ask him to do and does the opposite. Training your child from a very young age is best so they do not develop undesirable habits.

Remember, instilling discipline in your child requires time and focus. You have to be extremely patient.

## How Do You Learn About Discipline?

You cannot learn about discipline just by reading books, listening to teachers, or attending parenting seminars.

You will learn about discipline through experience. The more you try and make mistakes, the better. Practice makes perfect, and experience is the best teacher. You will get the hang of it.

Discipline has to be your way of life. It would be best if you practiced it from waking up until sleeping.

**"Discipline is vital in a man's everyday life."**

Instilling discipline in your child is a life-long process. You cannot achieve it overnight; it must be consistent and continuous. Over time, it will yield significant benefits.

Remember, you will always experience lapses. If there is a lapse, guide your child back to the routine.

Do not expect any transformation in your child unless you transform yourself first. My father always said, "You, the parent, must be a role model to your child." Your child will always follow what you do. So, if you live a life of chaos, your child will do too, but if you live a disciplined life, your child will follow you. Remember,

**A child will follow what he sees and not what you tell him to do.**

If you follow a discipline system, you will reap great results. Just make sure to be consistent. After all,

**"Self-discipline is the key to success."**

## Points to Ponder:

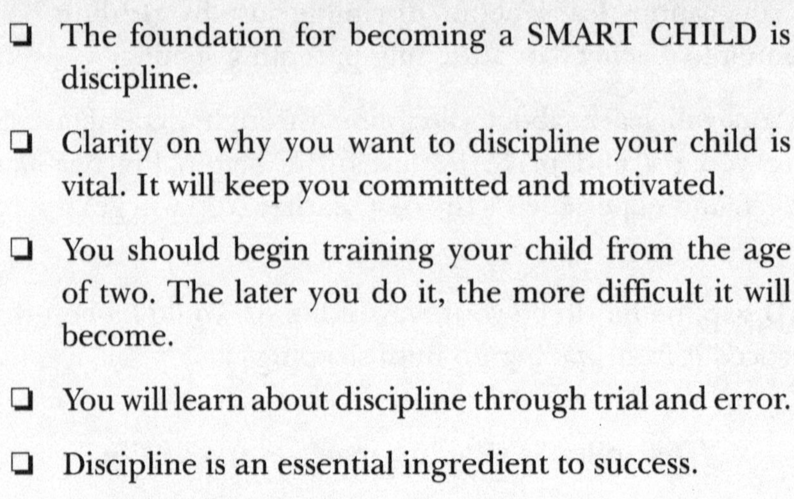

- ❑ The foundation for becoming a SMART CHILD is discipline.
- ❑ Clarity on why you want to discipline your child is vital. It will keep you committed and motivated.
- ❑ You should begin training your child from the age of two. The later you do it, the more difficult it will become.
- ❑ You will learn about discipline through trial and error.
- ❑ Discipline is an essential ingredient to success.
- ❑ Discipline will unleash the potential of your child.

# PART TWO

# THE RECIPE METHOD

SECRET #1

# Nourish Your Mind by Understanding the RECIPE Method

Have you assessed your child using the SMART CHILD Checklist? If you have not, please do so first. You must know what areas of your child's habits and activities need improvement.

After assessing your child, you need to understand the RECIPE Method so that you will know how to train your child. The RECIPE Method consists of six stages. It is a process your child must go through before transforming into a SMART CHILD.

In the following six chapters, I will discuss the whole process in detail so you can use this to guide your child through the different stages.

The figure illustrates the different stages your child must go through before becoming a SMART CHILD.

Let me begin by discussing the first step, “Develop Your Child’s Daily Routine.”

CHAPTER FIVE

# STEP 1: Develop Your Child's Daily Routine

- ✔ Do you sometimes wonder why your child is not doing well at school?
- ✔ Does your child have a daily routine?
- ✔ If so, does your child follow the routine consistently?

These are the three questions I ask every parent who wants to enroll in my tutorial center. My father told me that the first step to nurturing a SMART CHILD is to create and develop your child's daily routine.

Let me share the story of another student, Denise.

*I am the mother of Denise, a Grade One student studying at Colegio San Agustin, Makati. My daughter, Denise, had a big problem with her study habits. My husband and I are busy working and have no time to supervise our child's studies. Also, we do not know how to guide her.*

*My major problem is that I did not have a routine for Denise. So, I often found my daughter procrastinating and distracted. She always left her homework undone until the last minute, thus, affecting her grades.*

*Denise felt very stressed and anxious about her studies because she had no study habits. Whenever her teacher asked her for homework, she cried. The teacher called my attention to this matter.*

*I immediately contacted Teacher Mala, her tutor. She gave me valuable tips and told me what to do. I realized I needed a routine in place. I followed everything Teacher Mala said.*

*First, I sat down with Denise and talked about establishing a routine and how it would help her in the future. I also understood why Denise struggled with her studies. I discovered that she was easily distracted by toys, gadgets, and other things in her room. Also, she liked studying with others.*

*To help Denise, I decided to make changes. I started by making a list of all her assignments and tests. Then, I created a schedule and allocated time for homework, studying, and even breaks. I came up with the routine below.*

*After school, Denise returned home and ate. Then, she would go to the tutorial center to do her homework and study for tests or upcoming lessons. She reviewed her subjects even if she did not have a test. Upon returning home from tutoring, Denise watches television for 30 minutes before bedtime. She follows this routine from Monday to Friday.*

*On Saturdays, she rests. She plays computer games and watches television for an hour. She attends church on Sundays. After lunch, she studies again and prepares for Monday. She goes to bed early to wake up early on Monday.*

*I made sure her room was quiet and distraction-free. There would be days wherein I would sit with her during her study time to guide her if she was having any difficulty. I make sure I am there whenever she needs support.*

*I realized that parental support was vital. I have to check on Denise every day to address all her concerns. I guide her and explain things to her so that she will understand the reasons behind them and get her cooperation. This motivated Denise to excel at school.*

What did you notice about this story? Denise developed a discipline system when she followed the routine consistently.

## Definition of a Routine

A routine is a schedule or timetable your child follows every day until it becomes a habit. It needs to become your child's way of life.

Aristotle, a Greek philosopher, said:

**"We are what we repeatedly do. Excellence, therefore, is not an act but a habit."**

Aristotle believed it was essential to have a routine because it helps develop positive habits. You need to follow it strictly.

If you wonder why your child is not doing well at school, it is because she does not have a daily routine that includes studying. First, you need to establish your child's daily routine. It is the most crucial stage because it builds your child's foundation. Research has proven that habits influence a child's emotional, cognitive, and social development[2].

My dad always emphasized that before starting any endeavor, you must understand its importance and see how it will benefit your child.

So, let us see how Denise benefited from the routine.

2. Milestone Parenting, LLC, "The Importance of Teaching Children Routines", MilestoneParenting,http://www.milestoneparenting.com/productinfo/ImportanceOfRoutines.aspx, January 25, 2011.

## The Importance of Routines

The first thing Denise's mother did was to implement the routine strictly till it became Denise's way of life. When Denise's mother implemented it, she experienced a power struggle where both argued. A schedule solved it because Denise knew her mother was the boss and needed to follow her. Once this was clear, she followed her mother without resisting. The repetitive reminders diminished, and Denise completed her tasks on time.

Second, set the limits. Denise's mother defined the boundaries of routines. When Denise's mother put the limits, Denise knew what was and was not permitted and what her mother expected of her. Having understood this, she took charge of the tasks, feeling recognized and in control.

Third, a routine builds your child's foundation. Constant repetition helped Denise master the basics until it became a habit or her way of life. It molded her character and built a strong foundation along the way.

Fourth, a routine is predictable because Denise does the same daily tasks in the same order. Denise knew what would happen next. It helped reduce her anxiety, made her feel more secure, and minimized her fear of the unknown. It is because she knew what would happen next. She became more cooperative.

Fifth, a routine helps your child stay focused. Denise learned to finish one task to the best of her ability before moving to the next one.

Sixth, a routine teaches your child time management skills. Without a schedule, Denise could do whatever she wanted. With a plan, Denise knew how much time to spend on a particular task. She tried to finish all assignments within a specific timeframe.

The schedule taught her to be consistent with her studies, and things ran smoothly. Remember, consistency is the key. It also taught her the value of time.

Seventh, a routine builds your child's confidence and self-esteem. As Denise finished the task, she felt accomplished and confident. Also, it boosted her self-esteem. It made her feel safe, secure, and independent. When Denise became independent, she was less rebellious and easier to handle.

Eighth, a routine helps your child achieve her goal. The program was a roadmap for Denise to help her reach her goal. It was the implementation of the roadmap that allowed her to achieve her goal.

Ninth, a routine will teach your child respect. Denise's mother explained that she must earn respect. She can earn respect by listening, obeying, and following. Also, Denise learned to honor elders, time, and property. If Denise greeted elders, she respected them and followed the rules. When Denise followed a schedule, it taught her to value her and other people's time. If Denise took care of things, she respected property.

Tenth, a routine will teach your child responsibility. When Denise followed the schedule and finished her tasks on time, she became responsible and reliable.

Eleventh, when Denise followed a schedule, she knew she had to look forward to things she enjoyed doing. Denise understood there was a time for everything, and she could not do anything she wanted at any time. She needed to wait for the expected time for a specific activity which developed her patience.

Lastly, a routine reduces chaos during stressful times. Denise's mornings are chaotic. A morning routine sets the tone for her day. She had a morning routine and followed it because it helped her run things smoothly, especially during challenging times. It is a relief that Denise knows what to do under pressure.

An article titled *How 12 Highly Productive People Used The Power Of Routine To Achieve Greatness*, states that the secret to being a high achiever is simple. It is all about routine and focus.[3]

So, to succeed with routines, you need to create, develop and implement them consistently. You must be very patient, committed, and dedicated. Why? The initial stage is challenging. You will experience many setbacks. Lapses are normal. Dealing with these lapses will make you a better and stronger person.

Remember, routines can make or break your child's character. Therefore, you must be very careful.

## Components of a Successful Routine

When Denise's mother created her child's routine, she considered the following components. A successful routine has five essential elements. It must:

1. Have **a goal.** You must know what the outcome or result is.
2. Be **sure to communicate effectively with your child.** Explain to your child what will happen and what you expect of her. When things are clear, she will welcome the routine and gladly cooperate, especially if she knows she will benefit.

---

3. 3 LifeHack, "How 12 Highly Productive People Used The Power Of Routine To Achieve Greatness", Ash Roy, https://www.lifehack.org/articles/productivity/how-12-highly-productive-people-used-the-power-routine-achieve-greatness.html, Dec 19, 2019.

3. **Keep it simple.** It should have 3 to 5 steps to follow.
4. **Make sure it is easy to follow.** The routine should be simple so your child can follow it easily and enjoy it.
5. Be **consistent.** Follow it daily until it becomes a habit for your child.

Your child can follow the routine easily if it has all the above components.

What did Denise's mother do differently this time?

1. Make a schedule for Denise and post it where she can see it.
2. Require Denise to follow the routine for at least three months. Why three months? It is because the schedule must become part of Denise's life. I also wanted her to develop the habit of studying daily. Remember, consistency is essential when establishing a routine.

What did Denise's mother do wrong previously?

1. I found out that Denise followed the routine for only three weeks.
2. I also discovered that the mother wrote the schedule on a whiteboard, meaning Denise could erase it anytime.

You can see that Denise's mother failed to establish the routine here. **Parents must be patient, committed, and dedicated for successful implementation. Without this, it will never work.** She allowed Denise to follow the schedule and expected her to train herself. It also shows that Denise needs commitment.

After listening, I explained to Denise's mother that she needs to be 100% committed. So, she made sure that she implemented the routine consistently.

Now that you know the essential components of an effective routine, you can create one for your child or yourself. Here are helpful tips for creating a simple and doable schedule.

## How to Create a Routine

Once you have decided to create a routine, you must make a firm decision and start now.

Once you have decided to instill discipline in your child, you need to do these three things:

1. Observe your child.
2. Create a schedule.
3. Commit to implementing it.

Always observe your child. List the things you find pleasant and unpleasant about her. Next, write the schedule of activities you want her to do for the day.

1. List the tasks your child needs to do.
2. Write the approximate starting and ending time of the task.
3. Make sure you prioritize tasks and note deadlines.

4. Try the schedule. Make the necessary changes to make the plan smoother.

5. Test the schedule until it is just right.

Below is an example of Denise's schedule. You can create something similar for your child:

| START TIME | END TIME | ACTIVITY |
|---|---|---|
| 5:30 am | 6:30 am | Wake up, brush teeth, bathe, dress up, eat breakfast |
| 6:30 am | 4:00 pm | School Time |
| 4:00 pm | 5:00 pm | Have a snack and rest |
| 5:00 pm | 6:30 pm | Tutoring |
| 6:30 pm | 7:00 pm | Dinner |
| 7:00 pm | 8:00 pm | Finish projects or study |
| 8:00 pm | 8:30 pm | Watch TV |
| 8:30 pm | 5:30 am | Sleep |

As you can see, Denise's mother listed all the activities on the schedule. Denise follows this schedule strictly. It has helped her in many ways.

Now, can you come up with a schedule for your child? You may create your own.

In Secret #2, I have provided the necessary forms and instructions for you to complete.

## How to Implement a Routine

Now that you have created a routine for your child, you must implement it. Below are the rules you need to follow:

1. **Begin implementing a routine at a young age.** Ideally, it would be best to enforce the schedule from age two. The younger your child is, the easier it is to train. Establishing a routine is still possible when your child is older, but it will be more challenging.
2. **List down the routine steps.** The steps should be clear, simple, and easy to remember, understand and follow. It must be written on paper and posted in a visible place so your child can refer to it anytime.
3. **Your routine must be predictable.** The activities should be in the same order and time so your child knows what to do next.
4. **Include everything.** Your child's schedule should include all her activities. Make sure to allow enough time for each action.

5. **Follow the routine consistently.** Your child must follow the schedule daily until it becomes a way of life.

6. **Routines must accommodate sudden changes.** Your child's schedule should be flexible to accommodate unforeseen circumstances like typhoons, brownouts, or illness. When it happens, prepare her by explaining what will happen next. Be calm and assure her that everything will be okay. Then, return to the routine.

7. **Be patient, consistent, and persistent.** Follow the routine at all times, regardless of challenges. There is always a solution to every challenge. When you experience a challenge, be firm but kind, and you will find the answer. Remember, persistence is the key.

8. **Always include downtime in your routine.** Your routine should have entertainment. Remember, your child will only be young once and should enjoy her life. Enjoyment in moderation is allowed.

9. **Praise your child for her accomplishments.** Praise your child when she does something good or exerts effort to complete a task so that she feels motivated.

10. **Encourage your child to work independently.** First, teach your child the task and then allow her to do it alone. All you have to do is monitor and check.

Now that you know how to create and implement routines, you need to know the different types of routines you can develop and implement.

## What Kinds of Routines Can You Implement?

Different routines will help your child set the tone for the day. Knowing what and how each program will help your child is essential. Following are various routines you can establish for your child:

1. **Morning routines.** Mornings are crucial because they set the tone for the day. With a schedule, your child's day will begin smoothly and have an excellent start.

2. **After-school routines.** After-school routines will teach your child how to manage time, finish assignments and projects, and study for tests. It will also help build effective study habits.

3. **Dinner routines.** Families discuss their days, interact, and strengthen their bonds during dinner. Also, your child will learn table manners.

4. **Bedtime routines.** A bedtime routine prepares your child for the following day. The schedule must include brushing teeth and laying clothes for the next day. You must prepare your books, bags and materials needed for the next day so that your morning routine will not be stressful. Lastly, it must also include reading a story together and praying before sleeping.

Let's return to Denise. When the mother implemented the routine, she took the first step in nurturing her child to become a SMART CHILD. Why do I say this?

Establishing a routine may be difficult initially, but you must review it periodically and adjust the schedule to fit your child's and family's needs. It can be flexible or adaptable to your family's plans or something that works for you.

Have you tried to develop a routine for your child? If you have not, try setting one or two schedules. Stick to them for three months and see how things change for your child. Remember, do it consistently until it becomes a habit.

You will experience many challenges along the way, but you must face them and deal with them. Stay calm. It will help if you have patience, dedication, and commitment. Also, be firm but kind. Once your child sees you have all of these, she will follow. Commitment, dedication, and patience is the key.

Children will always be children. Experiencing a lapse is normal, but stay on course. It will help if you remind her what to do until it becomes a way of life. Keep trying until you succeed. Your efforts will pay off. Remember, FAIL means **F**irst **A**ttempt **I**n **L**earning.

Remember, a routine makes your child a SMART CHILD because it teaches your child to achieve her goals. In the process, she becomes more responsible and motivated. Also, your child will learn how to empathize with people.

Now, let us apply what we have learned. Do the following:

## ACTIVITY:

1. Create your child's schedule. The template is in Secret #2.
2. Explain to your child what is going to happen.
3. Implement the routine consistently for 30 days.

Please submit your child's schedule to stories@teachermala.com. I will check and give you feedback. After 30 days, share the story of your journey in implementing the routine.

Empathy is a skill every child must develop. It is the second area we must understand.

**Points to Ponder:**

- ❑ Step 1 in the RECIPE Method is Routine. A routine is crucial because it is the foundation of your child.
- ❑ You can implement different routines for your child: morning routines, after-school routines, dinner routines, and bedtime routines.
- ❑ Lapses are normal. When there is a lapse, you must know how to return to your routine.
- ❑ Dedication, commitment, and perseverance are keys to establishing your child's routine.

CHAPTER SIX

# STEP 2: Teach Your Child about Empathy

- ✔ Is your child only interested in himself?
- ✔ Is he also sensitive toward other people's feelings?

As a parent, how do I know my child is empathetic? These two essential questions will determine if your child is mindful of other people's feelings.

Empathy is a difficult skill to learn, but it is essential. Let me share a personal story about my mother before she passed on.

*My mother battled pneumonia for 15 years. In her last days, we were in and out of the hospital. It came to a point where she became exhausted.*

*She had so many food restrictions, like salty foods. My mother loved eating junk food, and I knew she missed out on many things.*

*One day she pulled a trick on me to get what she wanted. I ate pancakes for breakfast, and she asked if she could have some. I told her she was not allowed. She told me, "After I die, whenever you eat pancakes, you will remember me. You will feel sorry for not feeding me pancakes."*

*This incident made me realize I need empathy. So, when I spoke to the doctor, I asked him what I could do if my mother ate prohibited foods. The doctor told me to use a nebulizer three times a day. The doctor also made me realize that she is human and that I must make her happy. So, to keep her happy, I allowed her to eat whatever she wanted but in moderation.*

*Also, in her last days, she always asked me if I could care for myself when she was not around. Initially, I told her I would not survive without her. However, when I saw her suffering too much, I told her I would be fine.*

*Letting go was not easy, but I empathized with her. She suffered and held on to me while I realized it was time to let her go. I made this choice out of empathy.*

The above story is a classic example of an empathetic, compassionate, and selfless child. This child cares about her mother dearly and does not want her to suffer anymore.

The second step in the RECIPE Method in nurturing a SMART CHILD is to teach your child how to empathize with people. Remember, it is essential to respect and empathize with people.

## The Meaning of Empathy

**Empathy** is a translation of the German term *Einfühlung*, which means "to feel one with." It also means sharing the load or "walking a mile in someone else's shoes."

Empathy is trying to understand what the other person feels. When your child empathizes with someone, she puts herself in another person's shoes. She truly understands the other person's feelings and experiences and feels sorry for her. It makes your child more sensitive to the other person's needs or situation.

Children with no empathy and compassion are selfish and have a "ME first" attitude. They have very few or no friends.

There is a difference between empathy and sympathy. Empathy occurs when your child understands where the other person is coming from and understands the person and her situation more. On the other hand, sympathy occurs when your child feels sorry and pities the other person but maintains a distance from that person.

Some children have a high sense of empathy but difficulty expressing themselves because they lack social skills. It is because the emotional and intellectual quotients need to be balanced. As a parent, you must help your child and encourage her to develop her communication skills to express empathy.

## Importance of Empathy

It is essential to develop empathy in children while they are young. Empathy helps establish trust and builds connections, eventually leading to long-lasting friendships. When your child interacts with friends, She can relate to their feelings and experiences. Your child may even help them when necessary.

Empathy is essential to our society because it helps us build relationships with our community. Being part of a thriving and supportive community is the foundation of building meaningful friendships. In times of need, fellow community members may be able to help one another. The best way to prevent your child from developing an anti-social personality is to ensure she becomes a part of the community and interacts with others.

Empathy does not imply that a person must always agree with the other person's point of view. It means understanding their feelings and being open to finding a middle ground while sticking to your own principles.

It does not mean she does not have to pay attention to her personal goals, dreams, feelings, or preferences. Empathy means understanding how another person feels and wants.

In making decisions, your child becomes more considerate and compassionate.

Empathy is both a process of thinking and feeling. Your child must use her thinking skills to understand the other person's thoughts, feelings, reactions, concerns, and motives. Also, she must try to stop and think for a moment about what the other person is feeling and understand the person's point of view. Empathy creates the habit of thinking things through before acting on anything.

## The Stages of Empathy

My father always told me that it is essential to understand the different stages of empathy. Once you are clear, you can teach your child about empathy.

Empathy is the result of a combination of four basic abilities: paying attention (listening), inquiring (probing), digging down (investigating), and double-checking (clarifying).

1. **STAGE #1:** Paying Attention (Listening)

   Paying attention or listening is a skill your child can develop and master over time. She must pay full attention, stay calm, and listen carefully without judging. She must learn to focus on what the other person is saying.

   In my case, I observed and paid attention to how my mother felt. I did not want her to suffer too much.

2. **STAGE #2:** Inquiring (Probing)

   After listening, your child will probe further. She will ask questions and discover the other person's insights. Your child may ask questions that can be answered by yes or no, or she may answer open-ended questions.

Every day, I asked my mother how she felt. I asked her questions to get the necessary information about her feelings.

3. **STAGE #3:** Digging Down (Investigating)

   Your child must find out what happened after probing. If your child is empathetic, she will discover the other person's feelings. She will also learn how the incident will affect her and her innermost feelings.

   Sometimes, I tell my mother to describe her feelings in detail.

4. **STAGE #4:** Double-checking (Clarifying)

   After investigating, your child must clarify and check if her judgment is correct. It will eliminate any misunderstandings and clear up any ambiguities.

   I would double-check with my mother if she felt a certain way so that I knew her feelings and could act accordingly.

## How to Teach Your Child Empathy

1. **Please help your child describe her feelings.**

   Teach your child the feelings of each emotion. Ensure she understands and labels her senses to know what others think. Emotions such as "mad," "sad," and "happy" are the best way to start. They teach your child words like "disappointed," "surprised," "excited," "scared," "thankful," "left out," and many more. You teach your child to put feelings into words. Later on, as your child ages, it will also become easier to resolve identified feelings.

2. **Help your child read facial expressions and body language.**

   Point out facial expressions and other body-language clues to show emotion when looking at pictures with your child. You can make it more enjoyable by playing a game called "Feeling Theater." First, list some "feeling words" on paper. Choose one feeling and act it out using facial expressions and body language. Have your child guess the feeling you are trying to express. Then reverse roles. It is a fun way to teach empathy.

3. **Describe how actions influence feelings.**

   Explain to your child how actions can influence feelings by giving an example.

   Your child went to give Aunt Tina a gift. You noticed Aunt Tina's expression and told her that Aunt Tina looked so happy when she gave her the gift. Ask your child if she saw Aunt Tina's big smile.

   Also, explain to your child that behavioral mistakes affect feelings. For example, ask her, "Did you see how that little girl put her head down after the other children kept teasing her? How do you think she was feeling?" It will help your child develop sensitivity to other people's feelings.

4. **Provide empathy models.**

   Empathy teaches your child to be kind. When your child makes a mistake, such as knocking over a glass of water or breaking a cup, you can show empathy by being kind.

   When watching the news with your child, point out real-life examples of empathy. You can also look for historical models in your neighborhood or faith community. Then discuss appropriate situations that show compassion and explain it to your child so that she will understand.

You can turn movies, cartoons, and books into opportunities to teach your child about empathy. Do not limit your questions to "How do you think the character feels?", Instead, ask questions like, "In that show we watched, that little boy was enraged at his mother when he ran to the room and slammed the door. What made him so mad? Do you feel he had a reasonable reason to feel that way? How do you suppose his mother felt when he ran away and yelled at her?"

5. **Give plenty of practice.**

   Look for opportunities to practice empathy. Get your child involved in acts of kindness. Collecting clothes and household needs for a family whose house got burned down, cooking meals as a family to take to the evacuation center, or giving relief goods to calamity victims can help make empathy a habit.

6. **Discuss your feelings openly.**

   It would help if you discussed your child's feelings openly when correcting or disagreeing with her. Tell her exactly how you feel and ask her to do the same. It will enhance the communication between you both. At the same time, it will make you and your child understand each other better. Let me give you an example. Try to ask, "When you do not do your homework, it worries and concerns me. How does that make you feel when I keep nagging you to do it?" Ask your child how she feels. This way, both of you will understand each other.

7. **Use the emotional wheel when you teach your child about feeling.**

   My friend, Geniely Cruz, introduced me to the emotion wheel, a tool to help describe emotions. Below is a diagram of the emotion wheel. You can use this wheel to help your child express her feelings: bad, happy, angry, sad, fearful, surprised, and disgusted.

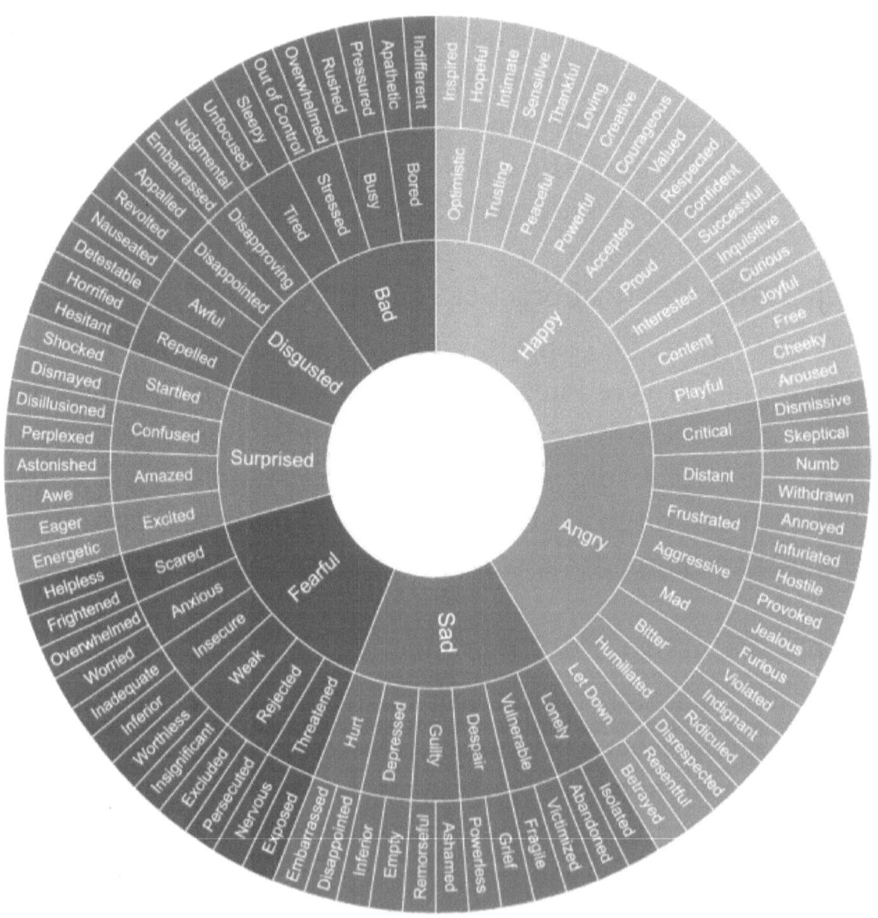


When your child feels a particular emotion, you can ask her to pinpoint what emotion it is. The emotion wheel will help you become very specific. Sometimes your child may feel two emotions or more, depending on the situation.

Using the wheel regularly will help your child recognize the changing nature of her feelings and identify triggers for specific emotions. You can address the sentiment immediately.

Empathy will make your child lovable and pleasant because it teaches her how to understand people's feelings. When that happens, your child will become charming and friendly. People will want to interact with your child, and she will learn to be sociable. Having friends will also motivate her, and she will become more trustworthy. The more friends she has, the happier she feels.

It is wise to teach your child empathy. As she develops empathy, her interpersonal and communication skills will improve considerably. She will learn to argue less and become more accommodating of others' weaknesses and imperfections.

Let us apply what we have learned. Drawing and playing a game is the best way to check if your child understands empathy.

**ACTIVITY:**

1. Ask your child to draw different emotions or act them out. (happy, sad, angry, disappointed)
2. How did your child portray the feelings in their drawings or acting?
3. What may have caused those feelings?

Please send a picture of your child's actual drawing or acting and share how your child explained the feelings to you. Please email it to stories@teachermala.com

It is wise to have patience, dedication, and perseverance when teaching your child empathy. Your child will become kind and compassionate. This world will become a better place to live.

Communication is a skill every child must develop. It is the third area we must understand.

**Points to Ponder:**

- ❑ Step 2 in the RECIPE Method is Empathy.
- ❑ Empathy is different from sympathy. Empathy understands where the other person is coming from, while sympathy feels sorry and pities the other person but maintains a distance from them.
- ❑ Empathy does not mean you agree with the person. Empathy means understanding what the other person feels and wants.
- ❑ Empathy makes your child lovable.

CHAPTER SEVEN

# STEP 3: Communicate with Your Child

- ✔ Can your child express his feelings?
- ✔ Does your child keep quiet when upset?
- ✔ Can your child get his point across?

These three questions will determine if your child communicates well. Do you believe that learning how to communicate with people is extremely necessary? Here is an actual incident that shows the effect of miscommunication.

> *My family had just moved to Jakarta, and we did not know the language. My father wanted the maid to clean the shoes on the rack because they were dusty and needed wiping. He asked my sister to look for the word "clean" translation in the Bahasa Indonesia dictionary. As instructed by my sister, my father told the maid to "chuchi zapatos" and left for the grocery store. "Chuchi" meant wash, so the maid washed the shoes.*
>
> *When my father arrived home, he was shocked. The maid washed the shoes. My father realized he had given the wrong instruction by using the direct translation of the word, but it was too late. Likewise, the maid took my father's word for it without confirming.*

The above example clearly shows that using the correct word choice is crucial. We cannot stop stressing the importance of communication because it enables your child to open up and express his feelings. A child who speaks well is generally happy.

In the above example, you will notice that if you use the wrong words, you will get a harmful or inaccurate outcome. So, be careful with what you say, how, and what you mean.

The third step in the RECIPE Method in nurturing a SMART CHILD is teaching your child how to communicate with others, an essential ingredient.

## The Meaning of Communication

Communication comes from the Latin word *communis,* which means common. Therefore, when your child attempts to communicate, he is trying to establish a common ground with another individual or within a group by sharing what he has.

Communication is a two-way process between two or more people. The sender and receiver exchange ideas, knowledge, feelings, information, thoughts, and opinions, fostering mutual understanding.

## The Importance of Communication

Communication creates meaningful connections between people. They get to know each other by interacting and exchanging feedback.

Communication helps you develop a strong bond with your child. Also, it will help you win your child's trust. When your child has a problem or something bothers him, you should be the first person he comes to for help.

Sharing information, like facts and ideas, is a way of communicating. It also widens one's knowledge and perspective on life.

Clear communication resolves conflicts and misunderstandings. Families with proper communication will have more peace and fewer misunderstandings.

We should not take verbal communication for granted. In the same way, we should recognize written communication. A simple billboard carrying a well-written message gets our attention and communicates a message while we wait in traffic.

Books become interesting when authors fascinate voracious readers with their words. Readers get so engrossed that they flip through the pages while reading until late at night without realizing the mode of communication.

Communication is more than word articulation. Using sign language to express yourself and touch to feel your environment is also a powerful mode of communication.

Communication aims to make things clear and bring both parties to mutual understanding.

Communication gaps happen when you take essential things for granted. You do not feel it because you ignore it or are constantly on the move. You will no longer have a vital connection when you realize this. Relationships strain when there is a communication gap. We are all guilty of it, primarily because of the daily grind and neglect of relationships. Bringing the connection back to its original state is sometimes challenging.

Children need constructive perspectives on two relevant topics like money and sex. Adult discussions often teach children that money is man's ultimate driving force. We ignore any communication about sex or hush it up as if it is taboo or sinful.

Without malice, a healthy discussion about money and sex is necessary for a child's maturity, wisdom, or survival. Today, countless people do everything within their power to attain both or either – to feel a false, misguided sense of control and well-being.

## Types of Communication

There are two types of communication: **verbal** and **non-verbal.**

**Verbal communication**

- **Oral communication:** Communication that uses speech to exchange information.
- **Written Communication:** Communication using written symbols – printed or handwritten.

**Non-verbal Communication:**

- **Body Language**: This includes facial expressions, eye contact, gestures, and touch.
- **Sign Language:** It is a language that uses visually transmitted sign patterns.
- **Paralanguage:** It is how we say something rather than what we say or mean.
- **Speech language:** This encompasses your surroundings while communicating (design and language). To communicate effectively, you use an implicit and careful choice of words and your environment to convey and impart a message. Also, it displays social status.

My father assumed that "chuchi" was the correct word in the above example. He should have shown the cloth to the maid so she would have wiped the shoes. It is one way of avoiding miscommunication through sign language. Remember, actions speak louder than words.

## How to Develop Good Communication With Your Child

1. **Spend time talking to your child.** Always find out how your child is doing so that if a problem crops up, you can correct it immediately. Your child may not understand certain things, so you must be present to answer his questions and explain things to him.

2. **Be approachable.** Let your child know he can talk to you about anything anytime. Assure him that you will not get angry at him. You will hear him out, weigh things objectively, and consider his feelings and opinions before saying anything.

3. **Do not judge.** Listen to your child. Refrain from acting like your opinion is the only one that matters. Discuss things with him and show him that his opinion matters too.

4. **Motivate your child.** Praise your child by expressing favorable comments about how you feel. Encourage him to do the same. You can reward him by hugging him or spending quality time with him. Do not motivate him by buying expensive things.

5. **Guide your child in making decisions**. Encourage your child to join you in analyzing options and making decisions. Teach your child how you came up with the decision by discussing your process and asking him what he thinks. Your child will feel that his opinions and judgments are valued.

Some children know what they want but get anxious or experience panic attacks when speaking in public due to self-esteem issues. To help your child express himself more freely, here are some practical suggestions:

## When Communicating with Your Child

1. **Focus on and pay attention to your child.** Listen intently. A wise parent needs to listen with an "educated ear." Hearing and listening are not the same.

   **Hearing** refers to the sense of sound. When you hear, you absorb the sound but do not understand or pay attention to what the person is saying.

   **Listening** means paying close attention, consciously assimilating what they say, or trying to understand what the other person is saying. Therefore, it is crucial to listen, not just hear your child.

2. **Respect your child as the authority in her life**. Do not dismiss what your child says as unimportant. Your child has experiences based on his circumstances. Allow him to express it. As you pay attention to what he says, you can guide him in making better decisions for the future.

3. **Try to understand the context** ("what happened") **and the emotions** ("how it affects") that your child is communicating.

4. **Acknowledge your child's emotional reaction by saying things like,** "That's frustrating" or "I think I hurt your feelings." If you are unsure what your child means, it is advisable to clarify your impressions. Repeat what he said and ask him if you heard him correctly.

5. **Know that anger is a default reaction of your child.** Your child may not necessarily be angry, but hurt or unhappy. He expresses it through anger. Please help him work through the situation and control his rage by helping him recognize his feelings.

6. **Learn to say "NO."** A wise parent strives to make his child understand that "No" can be positive. Your child should learn to say "NO" if he does not want to do something. It may mean he is protecting himself from danger or knows what suits him.

7. **Praise your child.** It can be as simple as telling him how fun it is to have him around. Be careful with how you communicate praise. Choose your words wisely. Saying, "You did a wonderful job, and I love you for that," could imply that you only love him when he does a beautiful job. Remember that compliments are necessary when your child puts in a reasonable effort. It will make him feel loved and appreciated.

8. **Hold family meetings or gatherings**. Communication and closeness are achieved by families meeting together. When family members meet, they must speak without interruption. You might want to consider setting meeting or conference guidelines. Prepare a short program with an agenda. Always end the session on a positive note.

9. **Do not lecture**. Lecturing is a power trip. Make the conversation short, sweet, and to the point. Also, add humor where appropriate. Feel free to point out your past mistakes as examples.

10. **Build trust.** Parents can communicate distrust without realizing it. Examples include when you finish your child's sentences. Allow your child to express his feelings. Ask him how he feels about himself, his life situations, and his peers. It will build self-awareness and assure him that you are listening.

## What to Do When You Face Miscommunication

Communication problems arise whenever your child needs to express what he feels. Failure to communicate will break relationships, and miscommunication will happen. When this happens, remember to do the following:

1. **Recognize that miscommunication happens to everyone.** Do not panic. Miscommunication does not mean your child is terrible; do not beat your child up over this and get stressed. These negative emotions will not help the situation.
2. **Assess the damage.** Is your child still talking to the person concerned? Is there any communication left?
3. **Make it right.** Refrain from dwelling on why something went wrong or the reason behind the miscommunication. Take the necessary steps to make things right between your child and the person concerned. Find out what will fix the relationship and take the appropriate action. It could mean renegotiating an agreement, apologizing, or clarifying issues. In the end, it's all about making the relationship right.

Establishing practical communication skills will help your child develop positive relationships, avoid controversies, and keep disagreements minimal. With open communication, there will be fewer arguments and misunderstandings.

Start communicating with your child early. Please do not assume your child does not understand what you are saying. You will realize your child can absorb what you are trying to communicate. It will greatly help during the teenage years when communication becomes more challenging.

Make sure you have a healthy relationship with your child. Your child's character will depend on your relationship with him. If there is a strain in the relationship, make it right. No matter what, he is still your child. There is nothing like harmony.

Once your child learns how to communicate, he will learn about concentration and commitment. These are two essential attributes of independence.

Communication will make your child pleasant and lovable. Once your child communicates well, he will become motivated, accepting, and happy. People will want to interact with your child because he can express his feelings. He will have many friends, and they will trust him. He will be happy.

It is advisable to have patience, dedication, and perseverance when teaching your child to communicate. Your child will experience harmonious relationships with the people around him, leading to a peaceful world.

Let us apply what we have learned. Playing a game is the best way to check if your child can communicate.

**ACTIVITY:**

1. Act out this scenario.
2. Your child has pushed his friend. His friend got hurt and is angry at your child. How will your child apologize to his friend? Have your child act out this scenario. Guide your child on how to handle this scenario.
3. Clue: Ask your child to say sorry.

Please share the output of your conversation with your child as you guided him in handling the scenario. Please email it to stories@teachermala.com

Now that your child can communicate well, you must identify interests or learning styles. You can make learning more enjoyable if you know the appropriate learning style for your child. Identifying your child's learning style is the fourth area we must understand.

**Points to Ponder:**

- ❑ Step 3 in the RECIPE Method is Communicate.
- ❑ Communication is a vital skill your child must learn.
- ❑ There are two types of communication: verbal and non-verbal.
- ❑ Start communicating with your child early.
- ❑ Establishing practical communication skills will help your child develop positive relationships and minimize miscommunication.
- ❑ When there is miscommunication, you must correct it right away.

CHAPTER EIGHT

# STEP 4: Identify Your Child's Interests or Learning Style

✔ Do you know your child's likes and dislikes?

✔ Do you know your child's learning style or interest?

Knowing your child's learning style is a must. These two questions will help identify your child's learning style.

Below is an illustrative example of a student whose learning style was incompatible with the teaching style.

*I usually see a gradual improvement in my students after a few weeks of tutoring. I saw no improvement in Daniel, a Grade 2 student enrolled in my tutorial center since kindergarten. He did all the assigned tasks, yet there was no marked improvement.*

*I decided to discuss the matter with my consultant. When he heard this, he immediately asked me, "Have you identified his learning style? All activities given to him should match his learning style."*

*I realized Daniel's activities needed to match his learning style. Since Daniel likes listening to music, we should give him more songs or music-related activities. After making modifications like giving him an "addition song" to listen to, we saw an improvement in him.*

The fourth step in the RECIPE Method in nurturing a SMART CHILD is identifying your child's learning style or interests.

Knowing your child's likes and dislikes is essential because it determines the learning style. Your child's learning style will help you identify the fastest way your child will learn. It may be visual (seeing), auditory (auditory), or kinesthetic (movement). Once determined, teaching your child will be enjoyable, less stressful, and more manageable.

Knowing how your child absorbs information will help build study habits. Also, the teacher's teaching style and your child's learning style must be compatible.

Daniel's story clearly illustrates that knowing and pinpointing your child's learning style is essential. It is because it triggers interest and can unleash your child's potential.

Daniel's mother did everything to help her child learn, yet she wondered why Daniel was not improving. She did not realize that one possible reason was that she was unaware of her child's learning style.

This section focuses on how to determine your child's learning style. You will know how to help your child with schoolwork and guide him with after-school activities and extracurricular classes.

## What Is a Learning Style?

**A learning style** is how your child best processes information or remembers things. In short, a learning style is an approach or method of learning.

There are three primary learning styles: visual, auditory, and kinesthetic. It follows that there are also three types of learners too.

## Types of Learners

### *1. Visual Learners*

Approximately 65 percent of the world's population are visual learners. Visual learners observe their surroundings, and they like art. Reading, watching, and looking are the methods they use to gather information. Visual learners enjoy screens, whether they be computer, television, or movie screens. They retain information found through visuals.

Visual learners tend to have photographic memories. They recall or remember images or visible details of places or incidents from the past. They visualize what they see in their heads.

They also favor illustrated explanations, charts, or graphic organizers. A visual learner can "see" ideas with his mind's eye and learns by watching and observing.

**Your child is a visual learner if he has the following:**

- A vivid imagination.
- An interest in painting, drawing, or crafts.
- A strong memory that relays visually-observed information.
- A good sense of direction and understanding of maps.
- An aptitude for reading and a love for books.
- A preference for writing things down.
- Recognition of people, faces, and places.
- A keen interest in observing the world around him.

If your child is a visual learner, the most effective way to give instructions is to draw a chart using colored baskets or folders. It will help you organize visually. If you find yourself verbally repeating the same thing over and over again ("auditory instructions"), try using "visual" Post-it notes because it will be more effective.

## 2. *Auditory Learners*

Auditory learners are listeners and talkers drawn to the sound and can easily follow oral directions. Approximately 30 percent of the population processes information best by repeating instructions. Some do it loudly, while others silently.

Auditory learners spell phonetically. Sometimes they have trouble reading because they cannot see well. These children learn by listening. They easily remember facts presented in a poem, song, or melody.

**Your child is an auditory learner if he has the following:**

- An aptitude for music and instruments or vocal ability.
- A tendency to sing along to songs or to create his song as he plays music.
- A solid verbal ability, primarily through repetition of words and phrases he has heard before.
- Listen and follow verbal directions.
- A love for talking and discussions.
- A sharp ability to notice sounds that others don't recognize.
- A perked-up mood when hearing music or dialogue.

If your child is an auditory learner, the best way to give instructions is to turn the instructions into a rhyme or song. Also, you can ask your child to rephrase the instructions aloud or learn from instructional videos and word games.

### 3. *Kinesthetic Learners*

Kinesthetic learners are physical learners who learn best by touching or doing things themselves. Young children depend heavily on this mode of learning. In short, a child "sees" by touching. About five percent of the population maintains this style into adulthood. They learn most effectively through physical interaction and have a strong sense of balance.

**Your child is a kinesthetic learner if he has the following:**

- An aptitude for sports, dance, or other physical activities.
- A tendency to fidget while in her seat – she may need to move while processing information.
- An inclination to use gestures when speaking or explaining things.
- A love of hands-on activities and play-acting.
- Enjoyment for writing, drawing, or handwriting exercises.
- Early physical development, such as walking, crawling, or sitting.
- Sharp hand-eye coordination.

If your child is a kinesthetic learner, he learns best through movement and manipulation. They like to discover how things work; some want to dismantle and reassemble items to see how they made the product. They often succeed in practical arts, such as carpentry or design. These kinesthetic learners comprise 50 percent of high school students and usually have difficulty learning in a traditional setting.

## Finding the Best Learning Environment for Your Child

It is wise to assess the environment and conditions in which your child learns best. Identify situations where your child learns best. Observe and see if there is a specific time of day when your child is most productive. You may answer the following questions to find the most appropriate learning environment for your child:

- Does your child work better while nibbling a snack?
- Is your child more responsive if the lights are dimmed or well-lit?
- Is your child happy with large groups?
- Does your child like to study in a quiet room or with music?

It is wise to ask your child to describe how he learns best. Experiment and see what happens. It will help you arrive at a "formula" or mix of conditions to help your child perform at his highest level.

Remember, what works for one child will not work for another. Each child has at least two learning styles: primary and secondary. Use and mix all three methods as often as possible to make your child's education effective.

Discovering your child's preferred learning style will spark interest in learning new things and give him a sense of achievement.

In Daniel's case, when we changed our teaching strategy, we saw that it sparked his interest in learning, and he started improving. He absorbed information quickly. It also diminished stress during study time. Today, he is excellent in Math and Reading.

Knowing your child's learning style is crucial to nurturing a SMART CHILD because it will motivate him to learn new things. Your child will also learn to be creative and happy.

It is advisable to have patience, dedication, and perseverance when identifying your child's learning style. It may be difficult initially, but you can accomplish it through trial and error. Once you achieve this, learning will be fun. Your child will absorb information quickly.

Let us apply what we have learned. Let us play a game called Truth or Dare.

**ACTIVITY:**

1. In this game, you need to prepare questions you want to ask your child or different activities you want your child to do.
2. Spin the bottle and see who it points to.
3. Let that person choose between truth or dare.
4. If your child chooses a question, let him answer it truthfully.
5. If your child chooses a dare, let him choose any activity from the three groups.

6. If your child chooses:
   a. Drawing activity – He is visual.
   b. Song – He is auditory.
   c. Dance – He is kinesthetic.

Please share with me your child's learning style. You can email it to stories@teachermala.com.

Once you have determined your child's learning style, you need to understand what perseverance is. Perseverance is the fifth step in nurturing a SMART CHILD.

**Points to Ponder:**

- ❑ Step 4 in the RECIPE Method is Interests or Learning Style.
- ❑ It is necessary to Identify your child's learning style because it triggers interest and can unleash your child's potential.
- ❑ Your child's likes and dislikes will help you determine his learning style.
- ❑ There are three primary learning styles: visual, auditory, and kinesthetic. A child has at least two learning styles.

CHAPTER NINE

# STEP 5: Teach Your Child Perseverance

- ✔ If your child finds an assignment difficult, does she try to answer it herself?
- ✔ Does your child read books to look for answers?
- ✔ Does your child use the internet to research information?
- ✔ Does your child ask for help until she finds a solution?

Perseverance is the key to become successful in life. These four questions will determine if your child has perseverance.

Let me share the story of my niece, Sonia, who was born with cerebral palsy. She failed in school, but her mother persevered in helping Sonia until she succeeded in her career.

*My niece, Sonia, was born with cerebral palsy, resulting in paralysis of the right side of her body. When my sister learned about this, she asked the doctor, "How can I help my child?" The doctor told her that Sonia had to go through therapy.*

*From the age of four, Sonia went to therapy. There was minimal improvement, but my sister did not give up. She always told me Sonia would reap the benefits later.*

*One of Sonia's biggest struggles was failing in Math. Throughout grade school, she failed Math despite my sister being hands-on in her studies.*

*My sister was worried because she wanted Sonia to have a career. She focused on Sonia's therapy and reviewed her daily school lessons. Over time, Sonia became dedicated to her studies. My sister saw an improvement but she was still worried because her daughter might not get college admission.*

*Sonia decided to take a teaching course in college. The school principal accepted her as the first special needs student because of her dedication and commitment.*

*True enough, she worked hard and excelled. Her mother guided her, and she was her biggest motivator. Sonia graduated as "top of the class." Her perseverance and hard work paid off.*

*Sonia found it easy to get a teaching job. Her employer was amazed at her dedication and commitment to her studies and work.*

Can you imagine what would happen if my sister decided to give up after hearing her daughter had cerebral palsy? It is because of her determination, dedication, and commitment that her daughter succeeded.

The fifth step in the RECIPE Method in nurturing a SMART CHILD is to teach your child perseverance. Sonia succeeded in life because of parental support. Her mother instilled the same values (determination, dedication, and commitment) in Sonia.

Perseverance is needed in all facets of life, whether in your career, home, school, or, most importantly, your relationships.

## The Meaning of Perseverance

Perseverance is the ability to stick to a goal despite the challenges, obstacles, or setbacks you encounter, and you believe your efforts will eventually pay off.

## The Importance of Perseverance

Perseverance is essential because it helps your child progress despite setbacks without giving up on her dreams and goals, even if she fails.

Perseverance can equalize things your child might not have. Your child may not be as intelligent, talented, or good-looking as others, but if she perseveres in what she does, she will achieve her goals.

Do you know who Beethoven is? Beethoven was a musician who became deaf, yet he made beautiful music that people worldwide still enjoy today. According to research, Beethoven showed a great deal of perseverance in music. It only reinforces that perseverance is a must for success.

Perseverance builds character in your child because it helps her overcome the challenges that arise without giving up. It makes your child more prepared to take on the next challenge.

Along the way, your child may lose focus and become obsessed with a particular goal. However, if you remind her of the bigger picture, she may become persistent and get back on track.

It will help to constantly remind your child of the bigger picture to dissuade her from not pursuing her goal. Instead, she must implement a strategy to track her progress and focus on her dreams, plans, and valuable yet attainable opportunities.

Your child must have the burning desire to achieve her goals no matter how slowly things progress. She will hang in there for as long as she can withstand it. She will develop concentration, focus, and commitment while enduring tough times.

It takes work to spot a patient and persevering child. Unlike other children, who easily give up for ease and comfort, a persevering child possesses the following admirable qualities:

- She gives up TV time to study more.
- She spends hours practicing a particular skill.
- She studies even when discouraged.
- She works hard to catch up after getting sick and missing a week of school.
- She finishes a challenging race and crosses the finish line.
- She saves money and makes lots of sacrifices to buy personal needs.
- Despite being home with frequent fighting and unhappiness, she excels at school.
- She tries something new for the first time despite the possibilities of obstacles and failure with sheer determination to excel.

## You Can Be a Model of Perseverance for Your Child

Here are some practical suggestions for training your child to be persistent:

- Wait as long as possible when something bothers you before venting your frustration.
- If something does not work as expected, keep trying until you succeed.
- Avoid losing your temper when something upsets you.

- Please continue to work on challenging projects until you complete them.
- Focus on something that often makes you lose patience. Process your emotions and take control of your responses.
- Work slightly harder or spend more time on a task you do not like until you develop an affinity for it.

## Some Activities Parents Can Do to Nurture Perseverance

- Work slightly longer or a few minutes longer on tasks you dislike.
- Record in your journal how you successfully handled all challenging situations you encountered.
- Write a poem about suffering: what you can learn from it, how to face it, and how to overcome it by transcending pain and suffering.
- Collect stories, poems, articles, or quotations about persistence.
- Brainstorm with friends about cures for "the blues."
- Read and learn from what Galileo (the famous astronomer) and other scientists endured from the opposition they faced.
- Find out from experts and trained people (e.g., counselors, psychologists, social workers, psychiatrists, and therapists) what help is available for people facing difficult situations.
- Create a skit that shows what to do when disaster strikes.

- Explore music's healing power.
- Explore exercise's healing power.
- Explore the healing power of plants and pets.
- Put extra effort into a challenging project and try to improve your skills like public speaking or learning a dance step.

## Tips on How to Teach Your Child about Perseverance

1. **Resist jumping in.** When you see your child struggling with something, do not offer help or jump in too quickly. Leave her alone and let her finish the task. If she cannot, she will ask for help.
2. **Start early.** Begin teaching your child about perseverance at an early age. The earlier you start, the easier it will be. Teaching teenagers to persevere is more challenging since they are more set in their ways and susceptible to other influences.
3. **Lead by example.** Your child will follow what she sees. Do not quit when things get tough because your child will follow in your footsteps. Set personal and family goals, track them, review them periodically, and adjust if necessary.
4. **Ask for help.** Teaching perseverance is challenging, yet you need to do it. Parenting is complex, and you may go through a roller coaster of emotions. One effective way of equipping you and your child with emotional tools is by joining parenting groups on Facebook.

**Let me emphasize:** Whatever your child decides to do, follow through. Along the way, your child will face challenges but can overcome them and achieve the goal. Remember, turning back is not an option. Do not quit. Perseverance is crucial to your child's personal development.

Developing your child's perseverance is very essential. If you do not teach your child to persevere, she will quit when she finds the task difficult. Your child needs to learn how to motivate herself. Giving up may become a pattern if she does not correct this attitude. It will be most beneficial to address this attitude.

Perseverance is critical to nurturing a SMART CHILD. At this stage, your child is friendly, motivated, accepting, responsible, trustworthy, creative, happy, lovable, and now dedicated. Perseverance teaches your child to be dedicated to her work and never give up.

You must be patient, dedicated, and committed to teaching your child perseverance. Initially, it may not be easy, but your child will become motivated once you achieve this.

Let us apply what we have learned. The best way to check if your child is persevering is to share stories of resilient famous people. Your child can also learn from stories about famous people who used passion and perseverance to reach long-term goals, often with failures or setbacks.

## ACTIVITY:

1. Read inspiriting stories like KFC's Colonel Sanders succeeding late in life or how J.K. Rowling's manuscript for *Harry Potter* was rejected 12 times before being published, showing your child how perseverance through failure can lead to great success.

2. After reading the story, make your child understand perseverance by asking questions and the moral lesson learned.
3. Record the session while asking the question. This is a good way to document your child's answers. When your child lacks perseverance, make your child watch this video.

Send a video of your child to stories@teachermala.com.

Teaching your child perseverance will prepare them to be independent. Once your child achieves this, the sixth and final step is to build self-esteem. Esteem is the sixth and last area we must understand.

**Points to Ponder:**

- ❑ Step 5 in the RECIPE Method is Perseverance.
- ❑ Perseverance means not giving up on the task, no matter how difficult.
- ❑ Your child must persevere to succeed in life.
- ❑ You can be a model of perseverance for your child.
- ❑ Perseverance is the key to success.

CHAPTER TEN

# STEP 6: Build Your Child's Esteem

- ✔ Is your child independent?
- ✔ Do you always have to remind your child?

These two questions will help you determine if your child's self-esteem has developed. It is safe to assume your child is independent since she has passed through all the stages. Independence is the key to self-esteem.

Let me share a recent personal victory that boosted my self-esteem enormously.

*After my father died in 2016, I weighed 96 kilograms. I was extremely heavy for a 5'5" woman and had health complications. The doctor gave me two options: to continue living and taking medication or to change my lifestyle.*

*After thinking about it, I made a decision. I realized I love myself, and I will take care of myself.*

*First, I listed the food I ate during the week. I realized I was overeating junk food and consuming too few fresh fruit and vegetables. So, I decided to eat healthier.*

*The next thing I did was remove sugar from my diet. Whenever I crave anything sweet, I use dates instead. I drink black coffee without sugar. Once I adjusted to this, I ate rice in smaller portions until I eliminated it from my diet. I did the same with bread and noodles.*

*As I changed my diet, I shed pounds, and my psoriasis gradually disappeared. I did one thing at a time until I adjusted to it and implemented the next till I reached a healthy lifestyle.*

*I did not expect any immediate change. I knew I had to go through the process one step at a time, so I made it enjoyable. Finally, it became a way of life.*

*Today, I have reached my ideal weight of 55 kilos and am happy that I am healthy.*

*Unconsciously, I applied the RECIPE Method to myself. As expected, it worked! This method is not only for children but also for people who want to improve themselves. I am a great example.*

My claim to fame within my immediate family is my unwavering commitment to whatever I embrace. You can overcome obstacles and rise above them. I always keep a clear and specific goal in mind. When I planned to lose weight and regain my health, I knew it would be very challenging from the very start. I had to wage war with myself, and I won!

Mala at 96 kg.

Mala at 55 kg.

Building self-esteem is the sixth and final step in nurturing a SMART CHILD in the RECIPE Method. It involves training your child to be independent.

After your child learns all the values, skills, and characteristics, she applies them gradually and starts doing things independently. It is a vital phase for you and your child. As your child develops independence, you will have less work to do since this is the turning point of her life. At the same time, you are helping her unleash her potential and build her self-esteem.

## The Meaning of Independence

**Independence** is the ability to do things alone without another person's help. An independent child does things on her own without being reminded. You must aim to develop this characteristic in your child. If you cannot do this, your child will depend on you for life.

Independent children display enthusiasm and optimism. They set their goals, do it repeatedly, and work to achieve them until they succeed.

Repetition is vital because it allows your child to acquire new skills and experiences. Along the way, your child will meet new challenges, exciting people and learn new techniques to face her challenges. Soon, she will enjoy achieving her goals.

Independence levels may vary according to her situation. Some children may be more independent than others because they learn self-reliance through past successes.

## The Importance of Independence

Being independent will give your child a great sense of self-esteem. Your child will build her confidence because she can make her own choices and do things independently, making her believe in herself. You become her number-one motivator because you are proud of her accomplishments.

Freedom gives your child a sense of accomplishment because it makes her feel more positive, worthy, and confident. It motivates your child to be more independent.

Independence encourages your child to explore and learn new things, generating curiosity and interest and automatically expanding her horizons.

## Letting Go

Letting go of your child is your first step to independence. It may be the first step but the most challenging step for you, parents. You are scared that your child will be unable to handle things or get hurt physically or emotionally.

If you hover around and fuss over your child, she will never develop independence. It will help if you let go at the right time. If you let go too soon, your child may feel insecure or unsure; if you let go too late, your child will be too dependent on you. Teaching your child to be self-reliant, responsible, and wise is critical.

### The Dos:

- Encourage your child to take baby steps toward independence. Begin by asking her to do her daily routine, like brushing her teeth and tying her shoelaces, until she gets the hang of it.

- Let your child spend more time in free play and allow her to experiment with her ideas so that she will learn to think for herself.
- Give your child responsibilities. When your child is older, ask her to help you with home chores like setting the table, watering the plants, cooking rice, etc. She will feel you trust her. Show her you appreciate her.
- If you see that your child is responsible, train her to manage her academic and social life but monitor her activities. If you feel she wanders off track, you must guide her to get back on track.
- Physical fitness and strength are essential parts of competence and self-reliance. You must encourage your child to do sports or outdoor activities.
- Allow your child to set goals but review them with her. If you feel she is taking the easy way out, but you know she is capable of more, guide her to set higher goals.
- Allow your child to be alone briefly because she needs some "ME" time and be at peace with herself.

Remember, you will not be around forever to hold your child's hand and protect her from all the pitfalls she might encounter. It is most effective to teach her to be independent and self-reliant gradually. Never underestimate your children.

If she cannot cope with or handle a task you assigned her, never label her as "stupid." Talk to her about her challenges and guide her on what she can do to complete the task. Encourage her to do a better job next time.

## Steps to Make Your Child More Independent

1. **Take things one step at a time.** Every time you do something for your child, do it slowly. Let her watch so she can learn how to do it alone. If you help her put on her socks and shoes, do it one step at a time. Show her how you turn the socks inside out and which side is left and right. Next time, let her put on the socks by herself and help her get them on. Next, show her how to tie shoelaces. Let her master one task before teaching the next one.

2. **Never be in a hurry.** Take your time when teaching your child a task. She may try to tie the shoelaces for the first time. It will take longer but it is fine. Do not get impatient while waiting for her to get it right. Restrain yourself from interfering but be around if she asks for help. When she does, guide her on how to do it and encourage her to learn until she can work independently.

3. **Watch.** Once you pass the stage of helping your child with every small task, you need to monitor her at all times. Tell her beforehand what she needs to do and how to do it so she does it correctly. Then watch. The more she does things independently, the more confident she will be with her newly discovered abilities.

4. **Help your child make lists.** Making a list is essential because it teaches your child how to organize her day. Initially, you can list all the tasks she needs to do. As she completes each task, ask her to cross it off. It will give her a sense of accomplishment and train her to become more capable, responsible, and independent. Guide her to make her list.

## Ways to Build Your Child's Self-Esteem

1. **Teach your child to fall asleep alone.** Spending an hour waiting for your child to fall asleep once she lies on her bed is unnecessary. Here are some ways to help her fall asleep faster:

    **a.** Take her to her bedroom and read her a bedtime story. Give her "kisses and cuddles" and tuck her into bed. Place a nightlight in her room to make her feel safe. Once she has adjusted, slowly shut off the light.

    **b.** Sit on a chair or the floor parallel to her bed so she can see your face. Your child may try to talk to you but ignore her or bow your head down because she is trying to fight off her sleep. Be strict and ensure you do not make eye contact with her, or you might give in.

    **c.** If she climbs out of bed, tuck her back into bed, or else she will do it every night, which may become a habit. She will try to get her way with this.

    **d.** Move farther away from the bed every night to give your child security. She will get used to it. Before you know it, you will be out the door. At first, it will be challenging, but if you stick to it, you both will get used to it.

2. **Believe in your child.** Let your child know you believe in her. Use positive words like "You are a smart girl. You can figure this out." to encourage her. Teach her to think positively by modeling this behavior yourself.

3. **Build life skills through a routine.** When your child wants to build life skills, she must do it repeatedly until it

becomes a way of life. So if you want your child to have adequate personal grooming skills, include brushing her hair and teeth and washing her face in her routine. It will ensure that she will do it repeatedly until it becomes automatic.

4. **Let your child make mistakes and experience consequences.** Life has many opportunities for your child to succeed and make mistakes. Do not be a helicopter parent by hovering over your child. Let your child make mistakes or fail because it will teach her a lesson.

   If your child makes a wrong choice, allow her to experience the consequences. It becomes more effective because it reminds her of the lesson she learned. For example, when your child extends her curfew by an hour, explain it clearly that she will lose her privilege of being out next weekend. It will make her think twice about staying late the next time she leaves.

5. **Make her do things independently.** Do not prepare things for her; instruct her what she needs to do and let her do it. Make sure she prepares for school by cleaning her bags daily, putting the right books, finishing her homework, and putting everything she needs. Be around to check in until she gets the hang of it. Also, allow her to pay at the cashier and count the change when grocery shopping. All of these will give her confidence in handling money and tasks.

6. **Let her speak for herself.** If your child has unfinished homework, let her deal with it. Please do not offer to do it for her. Let her talk to the teacher and explain why she has not finished her work. Be considerate if she comes home down and is worried. Explain to her why she needs to be responsible for her actions.

7. **Make sure your child knows how to protect herself from danger.** Your child must know how to protect herself from strangers. Tell her not to accept presents from strangers. Make sure she remembers the contact numbers to call in an emergency. Also, train her not to be intimidated by bullies, report the person to the proper authorities, and stay alert.

8. **Explain the value of things.** Always explain to your child the value of what you pay for or buy for her: special classes, bags, toys, and items she uses at home. Tell her you worked hard to ensure she has a good life. She must realize the importance of it all. It will create sensitivity in her towards the rest of the world.

Nurturing a SMART CHILD aims to equip her, with what she needs, to become a responsible, independent, and confident adult. It includes providing for all her needs, shielding her from danger, and nourishing her physically, spiritually, mentally, and emotionally.

However, many parents feel they should always be by their child's side. They fail to realize the real meaning of loving your child. Loving your child means teaching her necessary skills needed and not spoiling her. Giving your child everything will harm her.

Independence does not merely mean being free; autonomy comes with responsibility. It requires perseverance, dedication, and commitment. Nurturing your child to independence is complicated but achievable. As your child matures and makes decisions, you must allow her to express anger, apprehension, and doubt, if any.

How you respond to your child's initial efforts to attain independence establishes how she sees herself early in life.

You can help your child become responsible and independent through patience, perseverance, dedication, and constant communication. Remember,

**COMMUNICATION IS THE KEY.**

However, following up on her is still necessary because following through will keep your child on track. It is essential to monitor your child, especially in her formative years. Also, checking on her shows you love her. Remember,

**TIME = LOVE**

Spending time with your child is very important. Talk about doing things independently and explain to her the importance of it. It might take a lot of time, but it will happen gradually. Remember, change can never happen overnight but always in due time.

Building the self-esteem of your child is the last and most crucial stage. At this stage, your child does things by herself, without being rewarded, and has all the qualities of a SMART CHILD.

If you want your child to become a SMART CHILD, she must go through the RECIPE Method, the six stages that unleash her full potential. These are Routine, Empathy, Communication, Interests, Perseverance, and Esteem. In the process, she will develop ten essential values that every child must have: Sociable, Motivated, an Achiever, Responsible, Trustworthy, Creative, Happy, Independent, Lovable, and Dedicated.

Let us apply what we have learned. The best way to check if your child is independent is to assign the following chores.

## ACTIVITY:

1. Please have your child keep her toys in the proper place after playing daily.
2. Let your child pack her bag for school daily.
3. You can include these activities in her daily schedule.

Share your story on how your child did this independently. Send a video of your child doing these two tasks to stories@teachermala.com.

Once your child can do these two tasks, you are ready for the second step, Getting to Know Your Child Using the SMART CHILD TOOL KIT.

### Points to Ponder:

- ❑ Step 6 in the RECIPE Method is building your child's self-esteem. It is the last stage of the RECIPE Method.
- ❑ At this stage, your child does things independently without any reward.
- ❑ You need to follow through for your child to remain independent.
- ❑ The RECIPE Method keywords are Routine, Empathy, Communication, Interests, Perseverance, and Esteem.

SECRET # 2

CHAPTER ELEVEN

# Get to Know Your Child Using the SMART CHILD TOOL KIT

Now that you understand what the RECIPE Method is all about, the next step is to get to know your child. Below is a series of worksheets you need to answer. They are:

1. Get to Know Yourself
2. Get to Know Your Child
3. Worksheet on Schedule
4. The Smart Child Habit Tracker.

Let us begin by answering the first worksheet.

### Worksheet No. 1

It will help to be sincere when answering these worksheets. Think deeply before answering. The deeper your answer, the more you will benefit from it.

### Worksheet No. 2

It will help to observe your child first. List down the things you like and dislike about your child. Then, decide what values you want to instill in your child.

## Worksheet No. 3

For three days, list the routine of your child. On the fourth day, create a schedule and test it. Observe your child for 3 days. List down the things you like and dislike about your child. Then, decide what values you want to instill in your child.

**WORKSHEET 1**
**GET TO KNOW YOURSELF**

1. What are my beliefs about discipline?

2. Why do I have these beliefs?

3. When do I plan to take action?

4. How am I going to go about instilling discipline?

5. How committed am I?

    ____ Very committed

    ____ Not so

    ____ If things get tough, I will give up

| WORKSHEET 2<br>GET TO KNOW YOUR CHILD | |
|---|---|
| **Things I like about my child** | **Things I dislike about my child** |
| | |
| | |
| | |
| | |
| | |
| | |
| **Things I want to instill in my child** | |
| | |
| | |
| | |
| | |
| | |

| WORKSHEET 3<br>OBSERVE YOUR CHILD'S ROUTINE<br>DAY 1 | | |
|---|---|---|
| TIME | | TASK |
| START | STOP | |
| | | |
| | | |
| | | |
| | | |
| | | |
| | | |
| | | |
| | | |
| | | |
| | | |

## WORKSHEET 3
## OBSERVE YOUR CHILD'S ROUTINE
## DAY 2

| TIME | | TASK |
|---|---|---|
| START | STOP | |
| | | |
| | | |
| | | |
| | | |
| | | |
| | | |
| | | |
| | | |
| | | |
| | | |

**WORKSHEET 3**
**OBSERVE YOUR CHILD'S ROUTINE**
**DAY 3**

| TIME | | TASK |
|---|---|---|
| START | STOP | |
| | | |
| | | |
| | | |
| | | |
| | | |
| | | |
| | | |
| | | |
| | | |
| | | |

## The SMART CHILD TRACKER

Before answering the SMART CHILD Habit Tracker, you must understand why your child needs an assessment. An assessment will tell you your child's strengths and areas of improvement. A periodic evaluation will help you become accountable, track your child's progress, and plan your next steps on what your child should learn to nurture them to be a SMART CHILD.

## Suggestions on Habits You Can Develop in Your Child

### Area #1: Your Child's Daily Study Routine

1. Follow the daily schedule.
2. Keep the schedule.
3. No making frequent excuses.

### Area #2: Empathy

4. Greet elders from whom you need to learn.
5. Greet the people you know when you meet them.
6. Speak in a pleasant tone of voice.
7. Take care of your things.
8. Do not lose things.
9. Meet deadlines.
10. Be punctual in school.
11. Copy notes in the notebook.

12. Write notes in a diary.
13. Do all the assignments.
14. Bring the necessary books, notebooks, and folders to school.
15. Finish the tasks you assign him.
16. Ensure all you need for school is in the bag.
17. Finish all assignments.
18. Study the lesson for the day.
19. Be sensitive to other people's feelings.

**Area #3: Communication**

20. Communicate what you feel.
21. When upset, get your point across calmly.
22. Focus while doing the work.
23. No looking around while doing the work.
24. No stopping in the middle while doing the work.
25. No talking while doing the work.
26. No getting up while doing the work.
27. No complaining if you find the work challenging.
28. Ask for help if you do not know what to do.
29. Solve problems on your own.

**Area #4: Interest or Learning Style**

30. Watch television.
31. Read books.

32. Read instructions.
33. Look at pictures.
34. Look at billboards.
35. Listen to music.
36. Be sensitive to noise.
38. Follow instructions.
39. Hum to the tune.
40. Dance.
41. Run.
42. Play with friends.
43. Have at least one best friend.

**Area #5: Perseverance**

44. Welcome challenging assignments.
45. Research on the internet independently.
46. Ask for help if you cannot find a solution.

**Area #6: Esteem**

47. Work without supervision.
48. Work independently.
49. Plan your day.
50. Do tasks without constant reminders.

These are 50 habits your child needs to develop. Of course, we will only ask you to implement some of the habits. We invite you to do it one at a time and monitor it for 90 days.

Below are the instructions on how to implement the Habit Tracker. For this activity, you will need a calendar for the first habit. As the practices increase, you will have to make a tracker.

## HOW TO USE THE SMART CHILD Habit Tracker

Before you proceed, these are some guidelines you need to follow:

Decide on one habit you want to implement. For example, no talking while doing homework. Please read the instructions carefully. I hope this exercise will make a difference in your child's life.

1. For the next 90 days, before the end of the day, you need to review with your child if he did not talk.
2. If he did not talk, put a star.
3. If he talked, ask him why that happened and how he can do better. Please take note of it.
4. Then, begin from day one again.
5. Your child must complete 90 days straight for the habit to develop.
6. At the end of the 90 days, you can give your child a reward but nothing expensive.

It is an effective way of developing your child's habits.

Below is a sample of THE SMART CHILD Habit Tracker. I made one for 14 days. You can use this, or you can make your own. I usually use Excel or Google Sheets.

| **Habit** | **1** | **2** | **3** | **4** | **5** | **6** | **7** | **8** | **9** | **10** | **11** | **12** | **13** | **14** |
|---|---|---|---|---|---|---|---|---|---|---|---|---|---|---|
| No talking while doing homework. | | | | | | | | | | | | | | |

Put a check if your child did it or an x if your child did not follow it to track the habits.

# CONNOR & SHEILA'S

Daily Routine

SLEEP AT 9PM

**SHEILA WAKE UP AT 5AM**

- Exercise
- Breakfast with Dennis
- Prayer Time

**6:30AM CONNOR'S WAKE UP TIME**

- Fix bed
- Breakfast
- Change clothes

**CONNOR'S SCHOOL TIME 7:15AM TO 12:15PM**

- 7:15AM - 8AM - Sheila ligo / check emails
- 8AM - post morning message, greet birthdays,
- 9AM - message 10 peeps /learning session

**LUNCH BREAK 12:15PM TO 12:50PM**

- 1-1:30 PM Teacher Mala / write up
- 1:30pm to 2PM - ligo and play toys
- 2-3PM do assignments

**LEGO PLAY TIME 3PM - 3:30PM**

- 3:30 PM to 4PM answer 6 worksheets
- 4-5pm play outside (ball/bike/scooter) Sheila Call day
- 5-5:30PM drawing / colouring

**6PM LIGO TIME**

- watch Netflix
- read book
- dinner time

**7:30 PM RELAX TIME**

- Khan kids/ Code Spark / Word Worm / Happy Cheese
- 8PM play toys
- 8:30PM toothbrush and floss

The previous page shows an example of my student's mom's SMART CHILD Habit Tracker. You can design your own.

**Points to Ponder:**

- ❑ The SMART CHILD TOOLKIT helps you get to know yourself and your child.
- ❑ There are four forms you need to complete: the three worksheets and the SMART CHILD Habit Tracker.
- ❑ The SMART CHILD Habit Tracker helps you track your child's habits.

SECRET #3

CHAPTER TWELVE

# Motivate Your Child Using the HELP Method

Motivation is a powerful tool. When your child feels motivated, he will want to accomplish more. Let me share a story about how a parent motivated his child to get better grades at school.

> *Peter, a first grader, did not do well in the school year's first quarter, which worried his mother. I decided to talk to Peter to find out what the problem was. After listening to him, I realized Peter had so much potential. He needed more motivation.*
>
> *I talked to the mother, and I discovered Peter was playing Roblox. I suggested she limit his game time to thirty minutes daily. Instead, she should encourage Peter to draw or read books.*
>
> *Initially, Peter resisted and complained. As Peter's mother applied my suggestions, he gradually focused. Also, he listened more to his teachers, and his grades improved. Peter's scores were much higher during the second and third quarters of the school year.*
>
> *The young man has found another passion, drawing. Peter is now very motivated and studies alone.*

I told Peter's mother to implement the following rules and a reward system so Peter will follow:

1. Peter can only play or watch TV after completing his assignments and studying for his test.
2. Every time Peter gets a grade of 90% or above, he gets to eat his favorite food, watch a movie, or play an extra hour of computer games.
3. Peter can buy a book or a toy if his monthly test grades are above 90%.

When Peter's mother applied these strategies, she saw Peter's scores improve. He became motivated and focused. After a while, all of Peter's grades were above 90%.

As a parent, you need to know how to motivate your child. With motivation, your child will succeed.

Before you motivate your child, it is essential to understand the characteristics of a motivated child.

## Characteristics of Motivated Children

Motivated children are:

1. **Gregarious** – They enjoy social interaction and a lively crowd. They are friendly and adept at joining and leading when they feel comfortable. They hate to feel cast out in any way.
2. **Autonomous** – They solve problems, and they work independently.
3. **Conscious of status** – These children know where they stand and must maintain a solid and positive reputation.

4. **Inquisitive** – They are curious and must be allowed to explore and discover things without restraint.
5. **Aggressive** – They are effective competitors and want their views heard and respected. They are passionate justice fighters.
6. **Conscious of power** – They have a drive for responsibility, influence, and authority.
7. **Conscious of recognition** – They want to feel publicly appreciated for their gifts and accomplishments and will gladly respond to public acclaim.
8. **Conscious of affiliation -** They enjoy being connected to more prominent institutions because it brings fame.

## Meaning of Motivation

**Motivation** is the desire to work towards or achieve a goal. It does not mean your child is always excited and committed to his studies. It means he has decided to complete all assignments, even if it seems difficult or uninteresting.

## Types of Motivation

There are two types of motivation:

1. **Positive motivation** involves enjoyment and optimism about your tasks. Positive motivation includes rewards and reinforcements such as praise, certificates, medals, etc.
2. **Negative Motivation** involves undertaking tasks to avoid undesirable outcomes such as failing a subject; his parents may resort to negative reinforcements such as screaming, spanking, hitting, or threatening.

There are two types of positive motivation.

1. **Extrinsic Motivation** – Children are motivated by external rewards. For example, his mother will allow him to watch additional hours of television, play games, or eat his favorite food.
2. **Intrinsic Motivation** – Children are motivated by something from within, such as personal satisfaction, enjoyment, or fulfillment. There is no material reward involved.

## Comparison of Intrinsic and Extrinsic Motivation

| Intrinsic | Extrinsic |
|---|---|
| Results show after a long time. | Quick results |
| Children become more generous. | Children become more materialistic. |
| Rewards can be distracting. | Bribes or coercion are rewards. |
| Does not cost anything. | It may be costly. |
| Eager to learn more | Learn only when motivated or by force. |
| Very productive | Less productive |

Based on the above comparison, intrinsic motivation is more difficult to achieve. However, once you accomplish it, it provides better and longer-lasting results.

## The Importance of Motivation

**Motivation** is one of the essential key factors in nurturing a SMART CHILD. When a child lacks motivation, he attains mediocre or no results. However, when he is motivated, he achieves his goals.

Motivation is crucial because it drives or pushes your child to work harder and reach his goals. It will give him the strength to get up and continue even when things are not proceeding smoothly.

You cannot buy motivation. However, you can develop or cultivate it over time. To build motivation, your child needs an inner desire to change. It means he needs to work on himself, conquering fears and pushing forward to reach his desired destination.

Watching videos by Nick Vujicic and reading stories about Jessica Cox and other inspiring people are effective ways to motivate your child. Listening to inspiring music or motivational seminars are other ways that have a long-lasting effect on your child.

## Benefits of Motivation

1. **Motivation will get your child started.** When your child is motivated, he will work on the task effortlessly, and you will not need to remind him or force him to do the work.
2. **Motivation helps your child move.** Getting started is one thing, but maintaining momentum is another. Your child will always encounter obstacles that hinder success. He might quit if he loses interest or encounters difficulties, but he can overcome challenges and achieve his goals with proper motivation.
3. **Motivation gets your child to do more than what is required.** If your child is inspired, motivated, and energized about something, he will voluntarily do much more than necessary. He will not hesitate to go the extra mile because he knows he has a high chance of succeeding.

4. **Motivation makes your child's journey fun.** If your child is motivated, he will perceive the journey to success as enjoyable. He will achieve his goals and have fun along the way. Your child's motivation will enable him to bounce back and endure difficult times when things are not working well.

5. **Motivation helps your child finish the task and overcome his fear.** Your child does not know what is in store for him; he is reluctant and fearful of moving forward. If highly motivated, he will not allow fear to get in the way and will take the final steps to complete the task.

## How to Motivate Your Child

1. **Fill your child's world with reading.** You must teach your child how to read. Set a family reading time where everyone reads a book. Take turns sharing a book with your child. Show him that reading is essential to you by filling your home with printed materials: novels, newspapers, magazines, posters, and even mugs and placemats with words. Children learn to read by living in an environment "rich with words."

2. **Please encourage your child to make his own choices.** Allow him to choose his extracurricular activities or ask him to make simple decisions, such as picking out a dish for dinner.

3. **Show enthusiasm for your child's interests.** Encourage him to explore subjects that fascinate him. If your child likes cooking, teach him exciting recipes or challenge him to find five facts about food online. Make sure your child has everything he needs. My student loves playing with model houses in his free time. His supportive mother

bought him a Lego set. He continuously built different things but mainly houses. The mother is now the proud mom of a licensed civil engineer.

4. **Provide your child with play opportunities that support different learning styles, from listening and visual learning to sorting and sequencing.** Encourage open-ended play and other things, like blocks. Your child will develop creative expression and problem-solving skills by building and playing with various blocks and other educational toys.

5. **Come up with various activities and enthusiastically point out new things your child can learn.** Discuss how you find additional information, such as looking for gardening tips online or taking culinary classes on Saturdays. You can also choose an activity unfamiliar to both of you, such as playing tennis or speaking Spanish. You can schedule a lesson or watch instructional videos on YouTube. As parents, you can be the most effective model for your child. If you show your child that learning is a lifetime adventure, he will get the message and follow.

6. **Ask about what your child learns at school, not just his grades or test scores.** Even if your child does not do well grade-wise compared to other students, it is alright, provided he understands and improves. Do not discourage your child when he gets a low grade. Instead, ask him to explain what he learned at school daily in his own words. It is one way to check if he is learning. If you want to motivate him, you can discuss what he wants to know more.

7. **Ensure your child feels in control of his schoolwork by helping him organize his papers and assignments.** If he gets overwhelmed or discouraged, he worries more. Teach him how to organize his test papers and assignments. As he ages, things can become more challenging as his responsibilities increase.

8. **Focus on your child's strengths.** Your child may not have gotten an ideal score on his Math test, but he may have written a wonderful poem in his English class. Focus on your child's strengths by encouraging him to pursue writing activities. It will give your child the confidence to excel in English since he knows he is talented. Your child will feel optimistic about himself and will reinforce his other strengths.

9. **Turn every day into a learning opportunity.** Learning is continuous because your child learns new things daily and builds knowledge based on the latest facts. Please encourage your child to explore the world around him by asking questions and finding connections to help him make conclusions.

## Four Proven Steps to Motivate Your Child Using the HELP Method

1. **Help** your child by showing him what to do and how to do his tasks. Begin by telling him your expectations. Children usually comply if they know and understand what you expect of them.

2. **Examine** how your child does his tasks. Take, for instance, his homework. See how he does his homework. Make sure he does it without looking around, stopping or talking. If he prioritizes his studies, he can get high grades.

3. **Love** your child unconditionally. You want him to excel, but you need to accept and respect him for who he is. Make him realize there is more to life than achieving high grades and academic awards. Your child needs to exert the right effort first and accept his limitations, if there are any.

4. **Praise** your child. Please encourage your child by praising him for his good deeds especially when you see him doing acts of honesty, kindness, generosity, and selflessness.

## What Demotivates a Child?

Parents need to be mindful of things that can dampen a child's drive and enthusiasm:

1. **Never make your child your duplicate.** No matter how excellent your values are, you must realize that your child will likely look at life differently. Learn to look at life from his perspective.

2. **Saying things like "This is easy!" or "Anyone can do this!"** Instead, say something positive like, "You can do it if you work at it."

3. **Saying, "You are crying!"** Instead, ask, "Is there anything more you can do to improve your performance?" Discuss how your child can improve and help him spend more time productively.

4. **Never compare your child to other children.** It will make him feel like he constantly competes with his siblings, cousins, or other children.

5. **Always highlight your child's intelligence or essential abilities.** Explain to your child that complacency is harmful. Always tell your child he is competent. Please do not allow your child to feel incompetent because it is more destructive and may become a self-fulfilling prophecy.

## Steps Children Can Take to Motivate Themselves

Below are steps your child can take to enhance his motivation and awaken the power within to push him toward accomplishing his dreams.

1. **Set a goal.** Break a project into smaller tasks, making it more manageable, and ensuring each task contributes to the primary goal. As a result, you will find it easier to motivate yourself, as the size and the magnitude of the task will be manageable.

2. **Strive to finish what you started.** You must finish what you start. Develop the habit of completing tasks. Keep the momentum alive until the end, no matter how difficult.

3. **Socialize with people who have similar interests and are successful in their fields.** Surround yourself with successful people because you can share and learn from them. Also, it will keep you motivated.

4. **Never procrastinate.** Develop the habit of doing things now. If you don't, you will become lazy. Being lazy will lead to procrastination, and you will never complete the task.

5. **Emphasize persistence, patience, and resilience.** You will experience difficulties and failures along the way. When that happens, you must be patient and persistent in overcoming the problem. It will be helpful if you have the resilience to overcome difficulty.

6. **Read about your interests.** When you feel demotivated, read about something that interests you, it will change your focus, and you may learn something new and become motivated again.

7. **Constantly affirm that you can and will succeed.** Always look at yourself in the mirror and tell yourself you will succeed. Affirming yourself will help you develop confidence and stay positive.

8. **Be happy when you visualize your goals.** Take a moment to see the specific goals in front of you. It will help you attract what you want and keep you positive.

A motivated child has a definite path to pursue. Motivating your child is challenging. It is not a set-and-forget-it deal. It starts in infancy and continues throughout your child's life.

The more time you spend motivating your child while he is young, the less time you will spend solving academic and behavioral problems when he is older.

Let us apply what we have learned. Letting your child plan his reward is an excellent way to motivate him.

### ACTIVITY: Let your child plan rewards.

1. Start with small rewards., For example,
   Reward: Watch a movie
   Criteria: Your child needs to do his work every day, from Monday to Friday, so that you will allow him to watch a movie on the weekend.

2. As your child requests more significant rewards, the tasks need to be longer. For example,
   Reward: Go to Kidzania
   Criteria: Your child's tests need to be 90% and above.

When your child gets demotivated, please remind your child of the prize to motivate him.

Please share your story of how this helped encourage your child. Please email it to stories@teachermala.com

### Points to Ponder:

- ❑ Motivation is essential for success.
- ❑ Motivation will drive you to achieve your goals.
- ❑ Extrinsic and intrinsic motivation are two types of motivation.
- ❑ It is better to be intrinsically motivated because you will reap more benefits.
- ❑ The four keywords in the HELP Method of motivating your child are Help, Examine, Love, and Praise.

PART THREE

# WHAT PARENTS SHOULD KNOW IN THIS DIGITAL AGE

CHAPTER THIRTEEN

# Managing Your Child's Use of Gadgets for Effective Learning

The biggest struggle most parents have is to manage their child's gadgets. Many parents ask me, "Teacher, how do I manage my child's gadget use?"

Let me share a story about a student, Jonathan, who is addicted to gadgets.

*Jonathan, a Grade 6 student who is easily distracted, joined my tutorial center. It took him thirty minutes to finish a task, while the average child his age completed the worksheet in less than 10 minutes. He stayed at the center for at least three hours from Monday to Friday. When I asked him to read, he read without remembering details or understanding the topic.*

*I discovered Jonathan played with his gadgets after school instead of resting or finishing the homework.*

*At the scheduled time, he proceeded to the tutorial center for at least three hours. Then, he would go home and play with his gadget for at least two hours. He refused to listen despite being told he could play after finishing his schoolwork.*

*He barely passed because he did not submit his projects on time and got low test scores. If he had exerted more effort, his grades could have been higher in school.*

Jonathan was an ideal example of a child who lacked concentration. He could not focus because he was addicted to electronic games, a common problem among children in the digital age. The good news is that Jonathan can develop his concentration. Teaching your child how to focus is a crucial ability. Every child must learn this skill.

**Concentration** is focusing on one thought or subject and thinking deeply about it. Focus is necessary when studying, reading, or working because it helps you understand the topic faster and improves your memory. It will also help you finish a task quickly and achieve your goals.

## Different Stages of Concentration

A child's attention span is relatively short when young but is developed and lengthened over time. A three-to-five-year-old child has a three-to-five-minute attention span if he is doing an exciting activity. He may finish faster if the task is easy. He attends school, learns to sit down, and gains pre-reading skills. He also knows letters and numbers. Tasks such as picking up toys or clothes and placing things in their proper places help him expand his concentration. You must be very patient since a three-to-five-year-old's attention span is short.

Continued brain development enhances your child's concentration between ages seven to nine. Short-term memory and language skills improve over time. Soon, your child will recall and organize steps when doing tasks. He can cope with homework and sit still while watching a play or movie.

Your child's concentration and brain development increases from ages nine to twelve. By this time, your child can work through a project step by step. He can channel his concentration and motivation into sports, music, the arts, and other meaningful fields of interest.

## Factors That Affect Child Concentration

1. **Your child watches too much television.** Allow your child to watch television for thirty minutes to an hour daily *after* studying and doing homework. If your child watches TV before, he will think about TV shows instead of school assignments.

2. **Your child plays many computer games.** Allowing your child to play computer games for 30 minutes to one hour on weekends is advisable. The computer is like a drug that gets your child addicted to it. Brad Huddleston, the author of *Digital* Cocaine[4], describes how computer screens damage a child's brain. Brad Huddleston believes you must regulate computer use with proper guidance in today's educational environment.

3. **Failure to establish a routine. Never neglect your child's routine.** Everyone is guilty of this. To help your child develop concentration, create and implement the schedule consistently till it becomes a habit. Do not give up. Constantly fine-tune the programs to meet your child's needs. Also, continuously reflect on past programs and figure out what worked and did not work. Make the changes as needed.

4. **Your child is not interested in the subject matter.** Your child may become indifferent if the lesson is boring. To get your child's attention, the teacher must explain the subject matter in an engaging way to catch your child's attention. It will be helpful to supplement by creating

---

[4] Noah Webster Educational Foundation, "Your Child's Brain on Digital Cocaine: With Brad Huddleston," noahwebstereducationalfoundation.org, https://noahwebstereducationalfoundation.org/your-childs-brain-on-digital-cocaine-with-brad-huddleston/?fbclid=IwAR3ELO7AHhKfOvp_VA9zogZ4XcAasoufHEmyofJyY2WuFX3g_i3o7jMJz4w, 15 October 2022.

activities your child likes, finds exciting, and enjoys doing at home.

5. **Fatigue.** One of the most common causes of inattention is fatigue. Inadequate sleep causes fatigue. When your child gets excited and indulges in activities, he will get tired during the day. Once he is tired, he cannot focus. Ensure your child sleeps well at night to prevent fatigue and concentration loss.

6. **Improper diet.** You can link your child's concentration problems to an improper diet and unhealthy eating habits. Your child must eat healthy and balanced meals. Most children like sugary foods, but they are harmful because it makes them hyperactive and lose focus. Ensure your child consumes a balanced diet with sufficient vitamins and minerals, including iron and minimal sugar.

7. **Anxiety.** Based on my observation, anxiety causes depression. Due to inexperience, your child's brain may find it challenging to assess situations properly and assimilate stimuli from its proper perspective.

Anxiety happens when your child feels threatened, has estranged relations at home, has unrealistic parental expectations, has sexual fears, or has a broken friendship. You can help your child process his feelings, thoughts, and perceptions by discussing matters with him. You can also build a strong bond as you go along.

For concentration to develop, the mind needs training. Most people think concentration is a strenuous and tiring activity involving exertion and tension, both challenging and unpleasant. It is a misconception. Training is required.

## Nine Effects of Gadgets on Children

Below are the effects your child can develop from gadget addiction:

1. **Altered brain development.** The brain triples in size during toddlerhood and continues to develop until adulthood. Studies have shown that too many gadgets may negatively affect a child's brain functioning. They may even cause attention deficits, cognitive delays, and impaired learning.

    Instead of regulating gadget use, your child gives in to his impulsiveness and plays with the gadgets. Your child should sing, read, and talk rather than play computer games or watch TV at home.

2. **Obesity.** Your child spends more time playing on screens than outdoors in playgrounds and does not burn as many calories as he should. As a result, your child will become obese. It may lead to complications such as diabetes, heart attack, and stroke. Please encourage your children to walk, run, jump, and exercise, and make him understand that playing has many benefits. Therefore, teaching your children a healthy lifestyle is imperative.

3. **Violence.** Your child becomes aggressive after playing tablet games for long hours. Tantrums are the most common form of aggression among toddlers. As your child grows older, he confronts and disobeys his elders. So, instead of letting the tablets entertain your child, opt for coloring books, story books, or balls.

4. **Radiation exposure.** When your child uses a tablet for a long time, you expose him to radiation. You should keep your child away from these harmful gadgets to prevent radiation issues among children.

5. **Reduced interaction.** Your child spends less time talking to people. It hinders human interaction and prevents your child from developing communication skills. Toddlers struggle to communicate with their parents in a family setting because they surround themselves with toys. It distracts him from learning to communicate with the people in his surroundings.

6. **Sleep deprivation.** When your child gets addicted to playing with phones or tablets, your child will not get enough sleep. The tablet acts as a sleeping pill. Without it, your child will become grumpy and aggressive. Your child needs a good night's sleep. If not, he will lack energy.

7. **No exposure to nature.** Your child should socialize with other children in the park rather than stay home and play with gadgets. Exposing your child to nature is very important. Some overprotective parents find technology helpful since they know their children are home safely. However, they do not realize their child feels estranged from the natural world of plants, animals, lakes, and the sky. Children must throw a ball, hop, skip, jump, run, and call a friend by name, among others.

8. **Damaged eyesight.** Long-term exposure to computer screens strains the eyes. Experts say excellent vision depends on staring at things at varying distances. Research shows that your child will develop eye problems if he becomes addicted to computer games.

9. **Addiction to gadgets.** Addiction will grow if you continue to give in to your children's whims. Please do not leave your child at home with their devices. Instead, it will help if you expose him to activities that promote mental, physical, and emotional development.

Encourage your child to use technology in moderation. It is an emerging technology, and your child should learn about these advancements to protect him. Also, introduce him to playing outdoor games with children his age.

### What happens when you expose your child to too many gadgets?

1. Your child will develop a speech or language delay.
2. Attention-deficit/hyperactivity disorder (ADHD)
3. Learning problems
4. Anxiety
5. Childhood depression
6. Negative impact on the character

### What do you do?

You need to develop your child's concentration by developing his study habits.

## Tips on How to Develop Your Child's Concentration

1. **Set a routine.** Sit down with your child and make a schedule for tasks. It should accommodate entertainment, such as watching television and playing with gadgets, in moderation.

   As emphasized several times earlier, post the schedule where it is visible to your child. Make sure he follows the routine.

2. **Eliminate distractions.** Remove any possible distractions if you want your child to focus on his homework or other tasks. Turn off the television or anything that stimulates your child unnecessarily. Your child must have enough sleep. Ensure your child is well-hydrated, is not hungry, and has been to the bathroom. There should be no excuses for your child to get up during study time.

3. **Let your child accomplish tasks first.** When your child starts doing homework, ensure that he finishes it. It is not a healthy habit to leave it halfway.

4. **Ensure your child sits straight up in the chair while doing homework.** He should answer the work without stopping, talking, looking around, or peeping at his gadgets. If he does any of these things, direct him to his homework until he finishes it. If he wants to take an abrupt break before starting an assignment for another subject, allow him to do so.

5. **Allow your child to use gadgets or watch television for 30 minutes daily.** Ensure your child has some time for entertainment because it is essential to raising a balanced child. Remember, too much time spent watching TV and using gadgets will affect his concentration. He will not be able to focus.

6. **Make concentration a family goal.** When teaching your child to focus, the entire family must participate. The other family members should try not to distract him. From experience, the father usually diverts the child's attention. Most fathers allow their children to play with gadgets to compensate for lost time.

    Instead of playing with gadgets, it will be fun to play concentration games. Let me give you an example. While driving, ask your child questions about the signs you see while passing or what your child sees on the side of the road.

7. **Reward your child.** As your child's focus or concentration level improves, praise him for doing well. He will continue to put forth his best effort if he knows you appreciate how much he has learned and achieved.

## Creative Ways to Break Your Child's Gadget Addiction

1. **Engage in alternative entertainment or hobbies.** Put a **1,000** puzzle together or spend the evening watching the night sky. Spend time bird watching, sightseeing, or doing something fun. You can also try board games that spur creativity, such as Boggle, Scrabble, and Origami, and make scrapbooks for crafts.
2. **Change routines.** Involve your child in activities that do not require a mobile phone or other gadgets. Please encourage your child to explore creative activities like drawing, singing, or dancing to demonstrate creativity. Change the routine and ensure his free time is not synonymous with screen time.
3. **Do not keep digital devices accessible.** Mobile phones and other gadgets should not be within your child's reach. Monitor the time he spends using an electronic device or phone.
4. **Do not make it a habit to allow your child to learn from videos.** In this digital age, your children learn from videos. If you allow him to watch videos too often, you contribute to your child's gadget addiction. Instead, use

books for research. Most children find it difficult to read and write if they get exposed to learning through videos early.

5. **Encourage outdoor activities.** Outdoor play will help your child learn to play and interact with people. It will help build his motor and social skills.

6. **Engage in pretend play.** Play is the most efficient way to engage children in fun learning. It will also enhance your child's imagination. Children enjoy pretending to play. Start a fun game with your little one wherein she can pretend to be what she wants to be when she grows up. Your child will learn something, be away from gadgets, and spend time with you. Why not start now?

7. **Enjoy activity-based learning.** Your children enjoy playing with gadgets for fun and entertainment because they challenge them at every new level. Unlike mobile games, toys lose their charm after a few days. So, why not get your child something to play with that keeps him challenged every time he engages? You can subscribe to activity boxes delivered to your child every month so that he entertains himself for hours with this activity-based learning.

Young children often get distracted easily. It can be a big problem when your child grows up. As a parent, you worry about your child's lack of concentration or inability to focus on a task.

Let us apply what we have learned. Letting your child plan his reward is also an excellent way to limit his gadget use.

## ACTIVITY: Let your child plan rewards.

1. Start with small rewards. For example,
   Reward: Play computer games for 30 mins a day.
   Criteria: Your child needs to do his work daily, so you will allow him to play computer games for 30 minutes daily.

2. As your child requests bigger rewards, the tasks need to be longer. For example,
   Reward: Watch television.
   Criteria: Your child needs to review the lesson for the day.

When your child cannot focus, please remind your child of the prize to motivate him.

Please share how this helped limit your child's gadget use. Please email it to stories@teachermala.com

Limiting your child's gadget time is very beneficial. Your child will become less distracted, and his school grades will improve. Also, your child will be exposed to other activities and meet new friends. Your child may develop new hobbies.

### Points to Ponder:

- ❑ Your child must be limited in their use of gadgets.
- ❑ Playing with too many gadgets for long periods is harmful and addictive.
- ❑ Gadgets addiction affects your child's concentration.
- ❑ There are creative ways to break gadgets addiction.

CHAPTER FOURTEEN

# How Do You Begin?

**"Planning is the prelude to successful action."**

Training a child and establishing discipline at home is difficult, but you can succeed if you plan for it. Planning is the key. Always prepare before starting. Before implementing my shared method, you must prepare your child for what to expect so that he will be familiar. You might wonder, "What and why do you need to prepare your child?" If you want your child to cooperate, explain the process so he will not get anxious.

## Steps to Prepare Your Child

1. **Observe your child.** The first thing you must do is observe your child for at least a week. Please pay attention to what your child does, his likes and dislikes. Take note of your child's strengths and weaknesses. Do the worksheets in the Smart Child Toolkit.

2. **Visualize what you want your child to be.** List down all the qualities you want your child to have so that you will know what you want to happen. So, take a piece of paper and divide it into two. On one side, write "Things I like about my child," and on the other side, write "Things I do not like about my child." Visualize how you want your child to be. Write down all the qualities you want your child to have on a separate sheet of paper. Everything will become clear. Refer to the worksheets in the Smart Child Toolkit.

3. **Please communicate with your child regularly to guide him.** Spend enough time with your child to know how he is doing. Sit with him and assess how his day turned out. Also, discuss positive and negative things and what he can do to improve them. If your child thinks he did a good job, reward him. If not, talk about it and tell him what he needs to improve so he can do better tomorrow.

   Remember, communication is the key to a successful relationship with your child. You need to talk to him and communicate your expectations. If you want your child to wake up early, explain why it is essential to develop this habit and what to expect. It will lessen his fear of the unknown and get him to cooperate. It also gives him an impression of autonomy and involvement.

4. **Build your child's life skills through routines.** It will help if you create a schedule for your child. Once your child follows it repeatedly, it will become his way of life. In the process, your child will develop life skills.

5. **Accept your child for who he is.** You want the best for your child. You must realize that your child has his purpose and calling in life. He needs to achieve this to be satisfied. Help him achieve his goal, so you both can be at peace. Also, remember that no one is perfect. There will always be lapses because lapses are normal. It is a fact of life. So, do not be too harsh on your child. Forgive him if he did something wrong. If a lapse happens, do not panic but stay calm. Make him think about how to prevent this mistake instead of screaming.

6. **Pray.** Above all, pray for your child because prayer works wonders. You will be amazed at what God can do for your child. Miracles can happen. All you have to do is trust, let go, and see your child transform at the right time.

My father always said, "Remember, be firm but kind." Do not allow your child to sway you. As you go along, you will have to adjust. Always stay focused on the goal. Starting this journey is the most significant thing. Do not be discouraged if your child does not cooperate. Learn the ropes, and your child will eventually follow you. Treat this as a work in progress.

**Points to Ponder:**

- ❑ You must prepare your child before implementing the methods in nurturing your child.
- ❑ There are six steps to preparing your child. Remember these keywords: Observe, Visualize, Communicate, Build, Accept, and Pray.
- ❑ Be firm but kind as you train your child.
- ❑ Pray and never give up.
- ❑ You must begin this journey as soon as possible.

CHAPTER FIFTEEN

# Ten Do's and Don'ts for Parents

Some parents think training a child is easy. Please think again. Today, many parents must confront a significant problem: instilling discipline in their children.

For discipline to work, you must follow these ten rules. Failure to follow will make your efforts futile. Below is a detailed explanation of what you need to do and not do.

1. **Spend enough time with your child.** In today's economy, both parents work to make ends meet. Since both are busy with their jobs, they come home exhausted and want to rest. They hardly make time for their children.

   Spend quality time with your child. You must be very creative to find time to catch up and be with your children. Create an everyday schedule where you and your child can study and bond. If both parents are present, you can take turns, but if you are too busy, you can use the help of immediate family members. If you can do this, your child will do well at school.

2. **Monitor your child at home.** Do not expect your child to learn everything at school because this is a fallacy. You must realize that you must follow up at home. Please understand that your child attends school or the tutorial center for a limited time. The teacher will teach whatever she can during that period. If your child needs help understanding the subject, you must step up and follow up at home.

From experience, no matter how competent the teacher is, you must check if your child is learning. It can adversely affect your child's school performance if you do not.

3. **Do not spoil your child.** Please do not give your child whatever she wants because this may harm her. Never give in to her whims; be firm but kind in your convictions. Children will always try to manipulate you.

4. **Do not feel sorry for or pity your children.** Parents, both of you must be on the same page. Both parents need to agree on a particular opinion. If each parent has different viewpoints, the child might take advantage of the situation. In this case, your child may blame the other parent for not getting what he wants. As a result, both parents will fight, and one will give in.

   Do not let this happen. Do not feel sorry for or pity your child. You both should be on the same page and support each other. If you don't, your child will constantly manipulate the situation.

5. **Do not let anything stop you from making a decision.** When you tell your child, "Finish your homework, and then you can watch television," please keep your word. Mean what you say. Sometimes, your child will try to manipulate you to change your decision. If you give in, your child may no longer take you seriously. The danger is that she may also control her school teacher. I speak from personal experience.

6. **Do not expect the school or the tutorial center to discipline your children.** Parents and teachers must work together. They often play the blame game. Parents say teachers do not know how to effectively teach or

control students in the classroom. On the other hand, teachers say parents do not know how to discipline their children at home. Parents, you cannot expect teachers or tutors to discipline your child because this is your job, not theirs. You need to do your part.

Remember, discipline cannot be taught and implemented in school only. First, you must instill discipline in your home and then practice whatever your child learns in school. Make sure home and school discipline is consistent. If it is not, when your child returns home, she may unlearn what the teacher taught her at school and vice-versa.

7. **Coordinate with the teacher or tutor on needed measures.** Trusting your child's teacher or tutor would be most beneficial. Sometimes the teacher uses a technique you may need help understanding. Please understand that teachers do certain things for a reason. If it is unclear, clarify things with the teacher or tutor.

   Also, the teacher must introduce the lessons gradually and ensure mastery of the basics because it builds the essential foundation of learning. Some parents do not care about this. Teachers teach planned lessons even if the student hasn't mastered previous ones. They must check if the child has understood the earlier topic before introducing new ones because your child may get confused. When your child gets low grades, you will claim the teacher does not know how to teach. In reality, you must ensure your child has mastered the previous lessons to develop the foundation so she grasps the challenging topics.

   It is advisable to communicate with the teacher concerning such matters.

8. **Keep your commitment.** It is vital to resist the urge to give up if your child has difficulty doing the work or if you find it difficult to discipline them. Giving up is not the solution. Find the root cause of the problem instead.

   Giving up or quitting can become a pattern in your child's life. If your child encounters a problem, she may give up immediately. It will become a repeating cycle if you do not address this issue.

9. **Cooperate with teachers' disciplinary actions.** You may resist discipline by ignoring the teacher's instructions. You may unwittingly condition your child's mind so she will not listen to the teacher or refuse to do the assigned work. It can become counterproductive as it diminishes the teacher's authority.

   In reality, discipline is not only for your children but also for you. If you acknowledge the process, you and your child will grow and learn from the experience.

10. **Refrain from arguing about who is the house disciplinarian.** Usually, the mother cares for the home and the children while the father works. The father comes home late from work and hardly spends time with his children. When the father is at home, he wants to make decisions. He spoils his children with everything to compensate for lost time.

    The most effective way to address this situation is to discuss the matter openly and consider your child's well-being your prime consideration. Biblically, the father disciplines the family. The mother executes and upholds her husband's authority. The wife is with the child most of the time. Therefore, the husband should leave the decisions to the wife. It is because she knows what is best for the child. If you both fail to reach a mutual decision, you may have to seek the intervention of a family therapist or a child psychologist.

Building a healthy family life is crucial to your child's development. The last chapter will focus on healthy family life.

**Points to Ponder:**

- ❑ As parents, you make mistakes. You give in to what your child wants. It would be best if you were firm but kind.
- ❑ You must have an unwavering commitment to instilling discipline in your child.
- ❑ As a parent, it is your responsibility to discipline your child, but you must cooperate with your child's teacher in implementing disciplinary actions.

CHAPTER SIXTEEN

# Building a Healthy Family Life

Building a healthy family life is crucial. At any age, the environment in your home plays a huge role in your child's learning.

Your child's home learning environment includes everything you and your family do and the places your children can access. It will affect their development and learning.

When your child interacts with books, objects, and everyday experiences, they learn about the world around them. Your child must interact with people who provide love, security, encouragement, conversation, and positive role models. It will give them a sense of security.

A healthy home learning environment encourages children and young people to have positive attitudes toward learning, curiosity, and self-confidence.

## Straight Talk to Parents

Your child's primary training ground is the home; you are the first teacher. You are your child's most influential role model.

Children follow whatever their parents say, do, and think. It leaves an indelible mark on their offspring. As parents, we have the privilege of inscribing our teachings in our children's minds, who begin from a blank slate. We lay a solid foundation for positive behavior in a child or model the opposite. Let's take Brie's case, for instance.

*Brie, a six-year-old girl, was active and playful. Her teacher noticed that she suddenly became quiet. The teacher often caught Brie in her brooding mood and found it alarming. Brie attended her classes, but her mind wandered off.*

*Brie's mother attended the school's parent- teacher conference and admitted that Brie often heard arguments and shouting matches between her and her husband during late nights. Their family business is in terrible shape and might collapse soon, straining their relationship.*

It is imperative to raise children in a peaceful environment. A child feels lonely, insecure, and emotionally conflicted in a house where parents constantly fight. If your child feels that way, we cannot expect her to perform well in school or other productive endeavors.

Couples strive for happy and fulfilled marriages to make their kids happy and healthy. There are more troubled marriages today. Troubled kids are born where troubled marriages exist.

Conflicts at home are part of our daily lives and happen regularly. Problem-free families do not exist. Children must see rifts resolved and relationships restored and deepened. How?

Below are practical and doable suggestions:

1. When conflicts arise, you can change yourself for the better. You and your spouse have marked personality differences. Remember that you can't change your partner or spouse. Strive to accept your differences. Celebrate your similarities.

2. When love fades, and the urge to end it is strong, the scriptural command is to love anyway. As we grow older, we realize that marriage is more than an emotion; it is a conscious decision to keep the flame alive daily.

3. Never argue with your spouse in front of your children. If you have disagreements, settle them inside the room. It will help if you raise your children in a peaceful environment.

Children benefit tremendously when both parents have a peaceful relationship. Parenting becomes an inspired, focused, and delightful calling rather than an arduous chore.

## The Four A's of Effective Parenting

Parents must nurture their children by applying the 4 A's of effective parenting to raise safe, intelligent, and secure kids. These are **attention, appreciation, affection,** and **acceptance.** As parents, you must provide all these lovingly and wholeheartedly for your child.

1. **Attention.** Attention will make your child feel special and have a sense of belonging. Reward your child if she does something good or behaves commendably. Avoid yelling at her for misbehaving. Eventually, she might seek your attention by deliberately failing at school or starting trouble.

2. **Appreciation.** A sincere compliment can set the mood for your child's day. Praise your child in moderation. Too much praise can lead to over-confidence, while lack of recognition or appreciation may lower your child's self-esteem, leading to an inferiority complex.

3. **Affection.** Shower your child with physical and verbal affection. Affection is essential for her emotional growth. Never use affection as a reward. If you see misbehavior, correct it immediately. Let your child know you love her unconditionally.

4. **Acceptance.** Accept your child for who she is. Please do not compare your child to her siblings or cousins. Allow her to be different. Remember, everyone is unique.

Use the four A's listed above to build an encouraging environment at home. If your child studies alone, express your appreciation. If she does a chore without being told, praise her. Do not let positive things pass you by without acknowledgment. Commend her.

### Be Firm and Trust God for the Result

Parents' commitment is crucial. Parents commit, but when things become difficult, they lose motivation. They get tempted to give up.

Remember, if you give up, your child will lose. You should not stop training if you experience challenging moments. Be patient with your child as she goes through many highs and lows. Sometimes, your child will feel like she is passing through a dark tunnel. Remember, there is light at the end of the tunnel. You need to focus on that light.

In the beginning, your child will cooperate, and you will see significant improvement. However, your child may revert to her old ways, be uncooperative, and refuse to work after some time. She may also lose concentration. Your child may even rebel. It is a very crucial stage because it gauges your support and commitment.

I call this the "cleansing stage." At this stage, your child will undergo a process that will shake, challenge, and mold your child's character, values, and belief system. Your child will struggle and become confused. If you give up at this stage, your child will miss the learning process. However, if you remain firm and persevere, you will gradually see your child improve and transform. It is better to suffer now and reap the benefits later.

To nurture a SMART CHILD, you must be patient, dedicated, and committed. It will be more effective if you work hand in hand with your spouse, the teacher and your child.

Above all, trust God for things beyond your control. In the end, the result will be gratifying and fulfilling.

## FORMULA FOR A SMART CHILD

**NURTURING PARENT**

**+**

**PASSIONATE TEACHER**

**+**

**COOPERATIVE CHILD**

**=**

**A SMART CHILD**

## Points to Ponder:

- ❑ It is essential to build a healthy family life. A healthy family life plays a huge role in your child's learning.
- ❑ Use the 4 A's of adequate parenting: Attention, Appreciation, Affection, and Acceptance.
- ❑ For the discipline process to be effective, the teacher, parent, and child must work together.

CHAPTER SEVENTEEN

# A Final Word from Teacher Mala

I am grateful for writing this book. This book is a compilation of my two decades of teaching experience drawn from true-to-life experiences as a tutor in my tutorial center and my journey when bullied. After developing effective study habits and improving concentration, I have acquired the wisdom of an authentic practitioner. I hope this book will make a difference in your child's life.

Remember, discipline is a process. Once started, you must maintain it consistently. If you stop somewhere along the line, all your child's bad habits will slowly creep back in.

For the foundation of your child to be strong, the discipline process should be continuous till your child is in college. Remember, be patient, committed, and dedicated.

The Discipline Process

The image explains the various stages your child must go through to become responsible, confident, and independent. If your child has any lapse, your child will slip back to square one and will have to start the process from the beginning.

To develop your child's discipline, it is essential for you to **"Build A Healthy Family Life."** You can achieve this by implementing the four A's: attention, appreciation, affection, and acceptance. As parents, it is your responsibility to provide your child with these wholeheartedly.

Always teach your child to "**Believe and Achieve**." It is the most effective way to raise your child's self-esteem. Stop doing things for your child and let him do things for himself so that he will have a sense of accomplishment.

Use the four A's listed above to build an encouraging home life. If your child learns to wash the dishes, what a perfect chance to show attention and appreciation. If your child goes shopping for clothes, show acceptance. All of these positive behaviors will motivate your children to do their best.

Sometimes your children do poorly at school because they want to get more attention from you. Therefore, they misbehave. It will help if you give them the much-needed attention to prevent this from happening. When you give your child the required attention, he will develop a closer relationship with you.

Some children do poorly at school because they want to take revenge on their parents. Children can use failing grades to get even with their parents in response to excessive pressure to perform. Never compare your child to a sibling. It will make them think you are mistreating them.

Parent support is a must for your child to become a responsible and independent learner. You should coordinate with the teacher regularly. Follow up on your child daily. This way, if there is a problem, you can address it immediately.

Unwavering parental commitment is required. Initially, parents commit, but somewhere along the way, when they feel that things are becoming too complex for comfort or they do not understand certain things, they quickly give up. It should not be the case. If parents give up, their children will be at the losing end. Their child's discipline process will stop. Parents need to trust the process and the teacher as well. Sometimes, it is like passing through a dark tunnel, and you can see the light at the end of it. The discipline process is like that.

Dear Parents, if you want your child to have discipline, set the bar. You can help your child by being a role model. Your child will follow what he sees at home. Therefore, it is vital for you to **"Practice What You Preach." Always remember the essential Law of Discipline: "Results before Reward."** You must discipline yourself first before you can expect your child to follow.

Also, mean what you say. If you don't, your child will get confused and never believe you. Next time, your child will not take you seriously.

As you practice discipline, you and your child will pass through numerous cycles of ups and downs. Initially, your child will cooperate, and you will see significant improvement. However, after some time, your child will experience its downside. Your child becomes rebellious and will refuse to cooperate and work. He will also lose concentration. At this stage, parent commitment and support are crucial and needed. I call this the "cleansing stage." Your child's character, values, and belief system will be shaken, challenged, and ultimately molded during this stage. Your child will go through a struggle.

Your child is confused internally and does not understand what is happening. Sometimes, your child wants to do the task and sometimes resists it. It is not advisable to give up at this stage. Let your child continue the discipline. As things go forward, your child will begin to understand.

If you decide to give up at this stage, your child will not achieve the learnings of the discipline process and will not reap benefits too. However, if you become patient, committed, and persevering, you will see that your child will improve gradually.

This cycle will keep repeating until the college years when your child fully matures. The routine will be fully and wholly ingrained and imbibed. Your child has to practice it consistently throughout her life.

For your child to have a bright future, the three of you (you, the teacher and your child) must work hand in hand. The result will eventually be a responsible, independent, and disciplined individual.

I wish you success as you start your journey of nurturing your child into a SMART CHILD in this digital age!

To your success,

*Teacher Mala*

# One Last Thing...

After applying the strategies in this book, please answer the SMART CHILD CHECKLIST again. Let me know if you have seen a slight improvement in your child. I would love to hear all the successful ways you find to apply my strategies in parenting your child and your life. Please send me your breakthroughs and achievements. Nothing makes me happier than hearing from successful parents. I collect and study all kinds of success stories, large or small. When I get yours, I will send you a gift, an advanced training, worth Php 15,000.00.

You can also share your struggles if you are having a difficult time. I will send tips to guide you.

Be amazing,

*Teacher Mala*

stories@teachermala.com
help@teachermala.com

# Bibliography

Articlebase. "What is Commitment?" *creativeCommons.org*. 4 March 2022. http://www.articlesbase.com/internet-marketing-articles/what-is-commitment-1783017.html.

Blurtit. "How Important Is Perseverance in Life?" *blurit.com*. 21 July 2022. http://www.blurtit.com/q175787.html.

Larson, Christian D. "What is Concentration?" *Chest of Books*. 30 September 2022. http://chestofbooks.com/new-age/self-help/Concentration/What-is-Concentration.html.

Dr. Sears. "Discipline and Behavior." *AskDrSears.com*. 12 January 2022. http://www.askdrsears.com/html/6/t060200.asp.

Effective Communication. "The Importance of Effective Communication." *effective-communicating.com*. 15 August 2022. http://www.effective-communicating.com/importance-of-effective-communication.html.

English Coffee. "The Importance of Commitment." *vBulletin Solutions, Inc*. 18 March 2022. http://englishcoffee.com/showthread.php?t=9113.

Erupting Mind Self Improvement Tips. "The Importance of Self Discipline." *EruptingMind.com*. 21 October 2022. http://www.eruptingmind.com/importance-of-selfdiscipline/.

Ezine Articles. "The Importance of Being Independent." *EzineArticles.com*. 17 October 2022. http://ezinearticles.com/?The-Importance-of-Being-Independent&id=5626268.

Healthy Gamer. "Why dealing with emotions is a problem?" *Emotions*. 23 January 2023. https://wiki.healthygamer.gg/en/Emotions.

LdDPride. "Learning Styles Explained." *LDPride.net*. 25 November 2022. http://www.ldpride.net/learningstyles.MI.htm#Learning%20Styles%20Explained.

LeeHealth. "Are you addicted to social media?" 22 July 2022. https://www.leehealth.org/health-and-wellness/healthy-news-blog/mental-health/are-you-addicted-to-social media#:~:text=Using%20social%20media%20can%20lead,in%20neurological%20and%20physiological%20functioning.

Milestone Parenting, LLC. "The Importance of Teaching Children Routines." *Milestone Parenting*. 3 January 2022. http://www.milestoneparenting.com/productinfo/ImportanceOfRoutines.aspx.

Noah Webster Educational Foundation. "Your Child's Brain on Digital Cocaine: With Brad Huddleston." 15 October 2022. noahwebstereducationalfoundation.org. https://noahwebstereducationalfoundation.org/your-childs-brain-on-digital-cocaine-with-brad-huddleston/?fbclid=IwAR3ELO7AHhKfOvp_VA9zogZ4XcAasoufHEmyofJyY2WuFX3g_i3o7jMJz4w.

People Communication. "The Basics: What is Communication?" *peoplecommuncating.com*. 16 May 2022. http://www.people-communicating.com/what-iscommunication.html.

Smith, Mark K. "Howard Gardner and Multiple Intelligences." Infed. 25 October 2022. http://www.infed.org/thinkers/gardner.htm.

Suite101. "What is Empathy?" *suite101.com*. 14 June 2022. http://www.suite101.com/content/what-is-empathy-a94397.

Sasson, Remez. "The Importance of Concentration." *Success Consciousness*. 5 October 2022. http://www.successconsciousness.com/blog/concentration-mind-power/the-importance-of-concentration.

The University of South Australia. "What is motivation?" *unisa.edu.au*. 7 December 2022 http://www.unisanet.unisa.edu.au/motivation/Pages/What%20is%20Motivation.htm.

Values Education. "Perseverance." *Kunimitsu*. 9 October 2022. http://www.k12.hi.us/~mkunimit/perseverance.htm.

Values Education. "Respect." *Kunimitsu*. 13 March 2022. http://www.k12.hi.us/~mkunimit/respect1.htm.

Values Education. "Responsibility." *Kunimitsu*. 10 March 2022. http://www.k12.hi.us/~mkunimit/responsibility.htm.

Why Center. "Why is motivation important?" *WhyCenter.com*. 12 December 2022. http://www.whycenter.com/why-is-motivation-important.

WiseGEEK. "What is empathy?" *wisegeek.com*. 20 June 2022. http://www.wisegeek.com/what-is-empathy.htm.

WiseGEEK. "What is Independence." *wisegeek.com*. 10 October 2022. http://www.wisegeek.com/what-is-independence.htm.

www.ingramcontent.com/pod-product-compliance
Lightning Source LLC
LaVergne TN
LVHW041217150826
845673LV00001B/436